Fit to Surf

The Surfer's Guide to Strength and Conditioning

Ragged Mountain Press / McGraw-Hill

Camden, Maine • New York • Chicago • San Francisco
New Delhi • San Juan • Seoul • Singapore • Sydney

ROCKY SNYDER, C.S.C.S.

Certified Strength and Conditioning Specialist

• Lisbon • London • Madrid • Mexico City • Milan •
• Toronto

11 12 13 14 15   DOC/DOC   1 9 8 7 6 5 4 3 2 1 0

Fit to Surf was originally published in an earlier form by Emerson Publishing Company, Santa Cruz, California.

Library of Congress Cataloging-in-Publication Data
Snyder, Rocky.
   Fit to surf : the surfer's guide to strength and conditioning / Rocky Snyder.—1st ed.
        p.   cm.
Includes index.
   ISBN 0-07-141953-5
   1. Surfing—Training. 2. Exercise. I. Title.
   GV840.S8S69 2003
   797.3′2—dc21   2003007439

Questions regarding the content of this book should be addressed to
   Ragged Mountain Press
   P.O. Box 220
   Camden, ME 04843
   www.raggedmountainpress.com

Questions regarding the ordering of this book should be addressed to
   The McGraw-Hill Companies
   Customer Service Department
   P.O. Box 547
   Blacklick, OH 43004
   Retail customers: 1-800-262-4729
   Bookstores: 1-800-722-4726

Title page photo by Ron Brazil/Corbis. Photo on page 9 by Howard "Boots" McGhee (bootsite.net). All other photos by Scott Lechner. Illustrations on page 139, and 165 by George Arentz.

To Madison.
May you always feel the wind on your
face and the waves on your toes.

Contents

Foreword

by Kevin Miske Professional Surfer

Surfing has undergone phenomenal growth in the past decade. New surfers are discovering the lure of the ocean and the adrenaline rush of dropping in on a wave. Older surfers are returning to their boards to find the stoke they once had when they were mere groms. Young and old, new surfer or veteran, it seems like everyone is having fun with the sport.

Surfing is a strenuous sport that requires stamina, skill, and balance. Being a competitive surfer and rugby player, I've long recognized the essential value of fitness in high-intensity sports. We can no longer ignore the importance of improving our surfing through cross-training—fitness routines and sports activities that are in addition to surfing.

Historically, many surfers were true watermen who not only surfed, but also swam, paddled, body-surfed, and snorkeled. Perhaps they intuitively understood the benefits of cross-training: improved all-around conditioning and a body ready to take on the toughest demands of surfing.

Rocky Snyder's *Fit to Surf* comes at a time when training for surfing fitness is much needed. The new surfer may only get out in the water a couple of times a week, requiring him or her to find other times and places and ways to train. And even if you surf nearly every day, you should be running, stretching, and performing the exercises in this book to help make you a better surfer through better conditioning.

The illustrated exercises here are designed to increase strength, skill, and balance. In addition, they will develop your body so it's less susceptible to injury and so you can enjoy surfing even more. When you're physically fit, you can catch more waves, stay out longer without getting tired, and perform new and more demanding maneuvers. With a little time, determination, and focus you will see improvements in your surfing.

Good luck and aloha!

Acknowledgments

This book would not have been possible without the encouragement of family, friends, and clients who continually urged me to follow through with the project.

There are a few people, however, who were directly responsible for helping me see this work through to the end. My wife, Dana, broke me of my procrastinating ways. And thanks to Ramona d'Viola, for sitting through lengthy photo sessions. I would also like to thank Janice and "Wingnut" Weaver for introducing me to the world of surfing, and members of the M10 surf team for letting me use them as guinea pigs during the creation of this book.

Preface

I've been involved with athletics ever since I was a kid. I was born and raised in New England, where the seasons change abruptly every three months, so I found myself competing in many different sports. However, one sport I never experienced until moving to Santa Cruz, California, was surfing.

The ironic part of this story is that I spent my summers as a boy at Hampton Beach, New Hampshire, with waves that provide one of the best beach breaks in New England. To add to this, in the basement of my Massachusetts home was a classic longboard that had not been used since the 1960s.

I moved to Santa Cruz in 1991 and immediately fell in love with California. I was hired by a local health club and began my career as a personal fitness trainer, becoming certified as a strength and conditioning specialist (C.S.C.S.).

Before I get further into this book, I feel that I must make a confession and an apology. I confess that when I first encountered the surfing community of Santa Cruz, I thought they were just a bunch of people who did nothing all day but either surf or stand on the cliffs and watch the waves. It was not until I experienced my own love of wave riding that I learned this was far from the truth. Prejudices are based on ignorance, and I found that I was creating ignorant opinions based on a small, stereotypical group. For this, I deeply apologize to the entire surfing community. I thought surfers were nothing but loud-mouthed deadbeats. The surfers I have befriended are the most generous, caring, and friendly people I have ever met.

While working at the health club, I befriended a member named Janice Weaver, the wife of Robert "Wingnut" Weaver—who was one of the stars of the second *Endless Summer* surfing documentary. In the fall of that year, for a birthday present, Janice and Wingnut took me surfing at Pleasure Point (on the east side of Santa Cruz). Little did I know that this day would change my life forever.

We paddled out to a small point break and by the time we reached the spot my arms were completely thrashed. I had thought I was in great shape because I worked out at least two hours every day. But out here, old overweight guys and little wahines were paddling circles around me. I caught my breath as I waited for my burning arms to recover.

Wingnut turned to me and said, "Here comes your wave. Turn around and paddle. When you feel the wave pick you up, get up on the board."

That was the extent of his instructions. I started paddling toward shore as I felt the wave lift me up. Wingnut gave me a push down the face of the wave, I popped up on my feet, and I rode the wave straight in until it backed off fifty feet later. Wow! What a sensation! My first wave!

Since then, hardly a day passes that I do not stand on the cliffs and check out the ocean or listen to buoy reports. My tide book is always within reach. I quit my job at the health club to open my own athletic center at Pleasure Point, right beside the Santa Cruz Surf Shop. I live a hundred yards from the waves, and my quiver has grown to consist of nine boards, from a 6-foot-6 beauty to the 10-foot classic that used to sit neglected in my Massachusetts home. My professional work in fitness training and my love of surfing eventually resulted in my decision to write *Fit to Surf*.

I now train fitness clients each weekday during the mornings and later in the evenings; I surf in the afternoons and on weekends. I have become one of the people that I had made fun of in my ignorant years.

Introduction

People of all ages are enjoying the sport of surfing, and each year the numbers keep rising. Improvements in wet suits, surfboards, and leash cords are making it possible for people to head out into the waves just about any time they wish.

Most of today's surfers are prime candidates for fitness programs that can make them better surfers and help them avoid injuries. The young surfers of yesteryear are now adults with office jobs and long commutes. While their minds may still be young, their bodies have aged and are no longer up to the demands they used to place on them. But they still like to surf. Meanwhile, the young surfers of today are playing video games and watching surf videos, often less active physically than their mothers and fathers were at their age.

These factors lead to what has been called the Weekend-Warrior Syndrome, in which a person suffers a sports injury because he or she is basically sedentary during the work week but tries to play hard on the weekends. Among surfers, the result is sport-related injuries of the neck, shoulders, back, hips, and knees. Many surfers are "weekend warriors" who would benefit from a conditioning program designed to help them increase the strength, endurance, and flexibility needed to enjoy their sport to the fullest. This book fights the weekend-warrior syndrome by showing surfers how to condition themselves safely and effectively.

Workout programs, even at health clubs and commercial gyms, aren't usually designed for a particular sport. They may be good generic programs, but they are rarely created with the surfer in mind. I learned from personal experience that even years of strength training and conditioning don't help much with surfing in the winter swells of Santa Cruz, California. While fighting through overhead sets, after getting caught inside, I felt that I was out of my league. It was only after I looked at how I was training that I realized I was not training to be a stronger surfer, but that instead I was training more like a bodybuilder.

When we work out at our local health club, the programs that most of us follow focus more on a bodybuilder's routine than on ones specifically useful to a surfer. The typical program concentrates on a couple of muscle groups one day and other groups the next. Surfing requires the entire body to work together in a synergistic fashion, and the workouts should reflect this need and be more sport-specific.

In 1998 I was invited to vacation on a pleasure craft off the coast of Sumatra, in Indonesia. The plan was to spend two weeks traveling to fifteen of the finest surfing spots the world had to offer. Several months before departure, I set a personal goal of conditioning myself to be in the best surfing shape I could achieve.

Using knowledge I acquired through the National Strength and Conditioning Association, I analyzed the biomechanics of surfing. What muscles are used the most? What energy system do the muscles utilize? What are the most common injury sites? Once I figured this out, I created a conditioning program to get me to my goal. I trained hard with this program for several months, until I was in the best surf shape of my life.

Because of vast forest fires in Indonesia and immense regions of smoke, we had to call off the trip at the last minute. But the planned adventure had served its purpose: I was now truly ready for the winter swells of Santa Cruz.

Since then I have trained many surfers with this program, which is detailed in the pages of *Fit to Surf*. It's designed to be useful for all surfers, regardless of gender, age, or fitness level. You do not have to be a member of a health club for this program to be effective. Many exercises can be done at home or in the water.

The chapters of this book provide information on creating your own conditioning routine for surfing. They describe and illustrate exercises that contribute to strength, endurance, and flexibility. Sample conditioning programs for both gym and home are laid out in detail.

There are a few rules to follow for success with this surfing fitness program:

- Before beginning any new exercise program, it is strongly recommended that you consult your primary health-care provider.

- Execute proper form during all exercises and stretches. If the form is incorrect, different muscles must compensate—and the more compensation that occurs, the higher the potential for injury.

- If you experience dizziness, discomfort, or pain, stop immediately.

- The final rule: have fun!

Chapter 1

Creating Your Program

In creating your own conditioning program, start out slowly. Progress to more intense workouts only as your body gets accustomed to these exercises.

People who have exercised regularly in the past but have not exercised vigorously for several months, or even years, sometimes try to start a new exercise program where the old one left off. This can be dangerous because their muscles have deconditioned—even though their egos have remained intact. The chance of injury or extreme muscle soreness is greatly increased. It's important to start out slowly so the body can adapt to the new strains that exercise places on the body.

If any sharp pain is experienced while performing an exercise, stop immediately. The exercise may not be the right one for you. Check the description in this book of the exercise to see if you were performing it correctly. If it was performed properly, yet you still felt pain, omit that exercise from your conditioning program.

Following are some tips to help you develop an overall conditioning program that combines three cornerstones of physical conditioning: flexibility training, strength training, and endurance. All three types of training will then be discussed and illustrated in detail in the chapters that follow.

Flexibility Training

Flexibility is the key to injury prevention. Strength training and endurance programs have a tendency to tighten the muscles, so it's essential to stretch the body back to a balanced state.

Stretching exercises are used as warm-up for strength and endurance training. Most gains in flexibility, however, come when stretches are performed after such training. Be sure to take time at the end of each workout to properly cool down via stretching. The flexibility portion of your fitness program should be carried out daily, however, even if the other parts of the program are not performed on that day.

Strength Training

Strength training consists of relatively short bursts of muscular force anywhere between 1 second and 2 minutes. This type of training helps build size and strength in the muscles and conditions them to store more energy for immediate use. One to two days per week of strength training is considered a maintenance routine with little change in strength levels. Three days or more brings about physiological changes. Strength training sessions may vary between 10 minutes to two hours or more depending on the training protocol. I generally recommend 30 minutes to one hour, three to five days per week, to experience the physiological benefits of this kind of training. Other items to keep in mind concerning strength training exercises:

- When performing strength training exercises, start by executing one to two sets of each exercise selected.

- After exercising for a week, you can increase the sets from two to four per session.

- With most strength training exercises, perform between 8 and 15 repetitions in a set.

- If you cannot do an exercise with proper form for 8 repetitions, chances are the weight is too heavy.

- If you can do an exercise with proper form for more than 15 repetitions, the weight is probably too light.

- For exercises that do not incorporate the external resistance of weights (such as dumbbells or barbells), you can magnify the intensity by increasing the repetitions. Among these nonweighted exercises are abdominal and lower back exercises, push-ups, and pull-ups. Each set can include 10 to 30 repetitions.

It's a good idea to change your list of exercises on a regular basis so that muscles do not get too accustomed to the same movement. The greater variety you add to a strength workout, the greater the different number of demands you place upon the muscles—with the advantage that it forces them to adapt in a number of ways. Try changing the list of exercises each week or every other week. It's OK to repeat some of the same exercises, but be sure to alternate at least two or three of them.

Endurance Training

For endurance training, as with strength training, it's important to alternate among different activities. Endurance training includes such activities as swimming, running, and various forms of paddling. By alternating these various cardiovascular exercises, your body is challenged to meet many different types of movement. This can help reduce the chance of experiencing a plateau in training in which your body no longer develops at the desirable rate you've been experiencing.

In designing the endurance (cardiovascular) portion of your program, start slowly and progress to higher intensity in a methodical manner. Start with 10 to 20 minutes, two or three times per week, and add 5 to 10 minutes per session each week or add an additional day.

Many people gauge the intensity of their cardiovascular routine by their heart rate, using a target heart rate to monitor whether they are exercising at an ideal intensity level. Generally speaking, when you exercise at 60 percent of your theoretical maximum heart rate or above, desired physiological adaptations occur. Exercising at 100 percent of your maximum is not recommended. A range of 65 to 85 percent of the maximum heart rate is a safe range for most people. Anyone with medical concerns should consult a physician before establishing a desired heart rate for cardiovascular exercise.

To determine a target exercise heart rate, you can use a very simple equation, although the only factor taken into account is your age. Subtract your age from 220. The resulting number represents your theoretical maximum heart rate. Multiply that maximum heart rate by the desired exercise percentage (intensity) that you select (most likely between 65 and 85 percent) to find your target heart rate. For example, the theoretical maximum heart rate for a 40-year-old paddler would be 180; multiplying by a desired percentage of, say, 70 percent would result in a target exercise heart rate of 126. This is the simplest way to determine a target heart rate.

A better equation, the Karvonen Method, takes both a person's resting heart rate and age into consideration in determining the target heart rate. The best time to take your resting heart rate is in the morning, before getting out of bed. Count your pulse for 1 minute. This is your resting heart rate. The equation is as follows:

Maximum Heart Rate (220 – Age) – Resting Heart Rate x Desired Percent + Resting Heart Rate = Target Exercise Heart Rate

For example, a 50-year-old woman with a resting heart rate of 63 beats per minute wishes to exercise at an intensity of 75 percent of her maximum heart rate.

220 – 50 (age) = 170 (maximum heart rate)
170 – 63 (resting heart rate) = 107
107 x 0.75 (desired percent) = 80
80 + 63 (resting heart rate) = 143 (her target heart rate)

Use of a measurement known as the rate of perceived exertion (RPE) is a more subjective way to determine your desired intensity level. Simply put, on a scale from 1 to 10 (1 being very easy and 10 being maximal effort), how intensely do you think you are exercising? To determine your own personal target zone, warm up and then build to a submaximal yet challenged effort after a few minutes of endurance activity, such as paddling or running. Your heart rate at that point will be your target heart rate and will be between 5 to 8 on your RPE scale. Ideally a person should exercise between 5 and 8 on that scale.

Using both the Karvonen formula and the rate of perceived exertion may be a wise course of action. A combination of both approaches can provide a more accurate estimate of the correct intensity level for your endurance training.

Workout Programs

Chapter 9 provides detailed workout programs that are samples of the ones you can choose for your own fitness routine, including exercises for flexibility, strength, and endurance. One program is a 10-week plan for use at a gym or health club; the other is a 10-week program that encompasses the same conditioning goals but can be carried out at home.

Chapter 2

Flexibility Training

One of the most important elements in fitness, yet often the most overlooked, is flexibility. When your muscles are tighter than they should be, your body's movement is restricted. This makes any action require more effort. The more you stretch, the more flexible you become. Just by taking a few minutes to stretch before and after each fitness workout and before you surf, your body will feel better and function more efficiently.

The longer a stretch is held, the more likely it is that the muscles will relax and lengthen. Holding a stretch for 10 seconds is good, but 60 seconds is better. If any stretch causes pain, stop immediately and omit that stretch from the program for the time being. Not all stretches are for everybody. Perform those stretches that feel good. The following stretches can be performed daily.

Chapter 9 provides detailed workout programs that incorporate these various stretches.

Crossed Knee Lift

1. Lie on the floor face up, with your arms straight out from the sides of your body and palms down.

2. Cross one ankle over the opposite knee.

3. Lift the knee up directly above the hip and hold for at least 15 seconds.

4. Repeat using the opposite leg.

Benefit: Stretches hip muscles that tighten, and strengthens other hip muscles that weaken, when surfing.

Crossover Twist

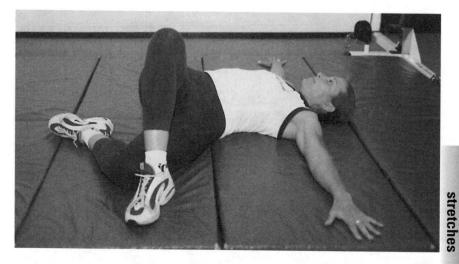

1. Lie on the floor face up, with your arms straight out from the sides of your body and palms down.

2. Bend the knees at right angles so your feet are flat on the floor.

3. Cross one ankle over the opposite knee.

4. Keeping shoulders and arms on the floor, rotate the leg and the crossed foot over to the side until both rest on the floor.

5. The knee that is not on the floor should point up to the ceiling.

6. Hold for at least 15 seconds.

7. Repeat using the opposite leg and foot.

Benefit: Stretches tight hip and lower back muscles and enhances torso rotation.

Mad Cat Stretch

stretches

1. Support your body on all fours, with your hands below the shoulders and your knees below the hips. [1]

2. Breathe out as you arch your back upward. [2]

3. Breathe in as you bow your back downward.

4. Move your head in the opposite direction of the back.

5. The movement should be continuous, without pausing at the top or the bottom.

Benefit: Promotes better movement in the back, shoulders, and hips.

Chest and Shoulder Stretch

1. Stand with your feet parallel and knees slightly bent.

2. Clasp both hands together, with fingers interlocked behind your back.

3. Straighten both arms and push your hands away from your body.

4. Keep your body upright, making sure your torso does not bend forward.

Benefit: Stretches muscles that tighten when paddling.

stretches

Seated Torso Twist

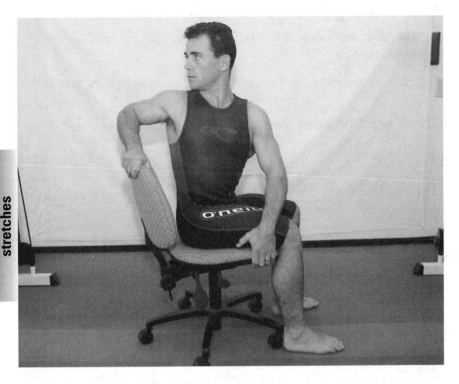

1. Sit in a chair, with your knees parallel and at right angles to the hips and ankles. Your feet should point straight ahead.

2. Remain in a tall seated posture as you twist your torso to the right as you reach around to the top of the backrest with your right hand.

3. Hold on to the bottom-right corner of the seat with your left hand.

4. Keep hips and legs facing forward so the rotation occurs in the spine and torso.

5. Hold for 10 seconds to 1 minute before switching sides.

Benefit: Improves torso and lower back flexibility.

Simple Twist

1. In a seated position, bring your right leg behind your body by bending at the right knee.

2. Place the sole of your left foot against the top of your right knee and thigh.

3. Remain in a tall seated position as you reach back behind your body with your left hand and twist your torso to the left.

4. Keep your left hand anchored to the floor and bring your right hand to the left knee to assist in the twisting.

5. Hold for 10 seconds to 1 minute before switching sides.

Benefit: Improves flexibility of the spine, waist, and front side of the hip.

Seated Lower-Back Stretch

1. In a tall seated posture, straighten your right leg in front of your body, with the foot pointing to the ceiling.

2. Bend at the left knee and cross the left foot over the right leg and down to the floor so that the foot can be pulled flat toward your groin.

3. Place your left elbow against the inside of your left knee as you reach around with your right arm and then anchor it to the floor behind your body.

4. Hold for 10 seconds to 1 minute before switching sides.

Benefit: Improves flexibility to each side of the lower back.
Note: For a variation of this stretch, carry out the exercise without crossing one leg over the other, or rotate in the opposite direction.

Bar Hang

1. Use a pull-up bar or other sturdy object from which to hang.

2. Grab the bar outside of shoulder-width.

3. Gently relax your shoulders as your body sinks toward the ground.

4. Hold for 10 seconds to 1 minute.

Benefit: Reduces spinal compression, stretches shoulders and back, and improves grip strength.

Crossed Arm Stretch

stretches

1. With elbows bent, cross one arm above the other so one elbow is nestled in the pit of the opposite arm.

2. With the hand of the lower arm, grasp the opposite wrist, with both arms pointing upward.

3. Pull both elbows downward and hold for at least 15 seconds.

4. Switch arms and perform the same stretch.

Benefit: Stretches neck and shoulder muscles that tighten when supporting your head during paddling.

Arm Circles

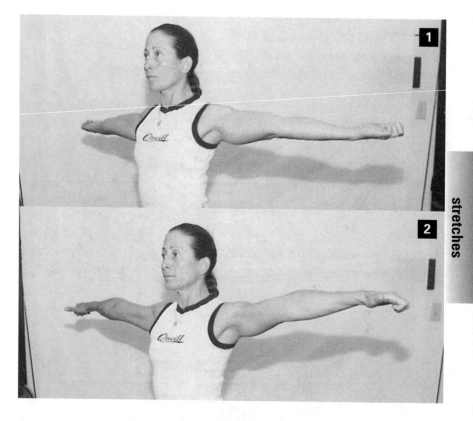

1. Extend your arms out from the sides of your body at shoulder height.

2. Keep your shoulder blades pinched together as your arms make 6-inch circles backward, with palms face up. [1]

3. Flip your palms down and reverse the circle direction. [2]

4. Keep your body as still as possible, with movement occurring only at the shoulder joint.

Benefit: Promotes proper shoulder movement for paddling.

Shoulder Pivots

1. Curl your fingers in toward the palms, and place your knuckles against your temples, palms faced forward and thumbs down. [1]

2. Keep knuckle contact with the temples at all times.

3. Pull your elbows together until they touch. [2]

4. Then pull your elbows apart as far as possible.

Benefit: Promotes proper shoulder function when paddling.

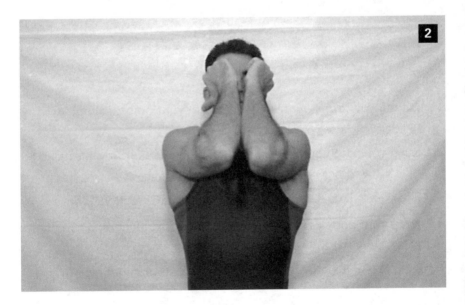

Lateral Neck Stretch

1. Place your left arm behind your back, with the elbow bent.

2. With your right hand, gently pull the left side of your head toward the right shoulder.

3. Repeat using opposite arms.

Benefit: Stretches neck muscles that tighten when you are paddling.

stretches

Forward Neck Stretch

1. Stand with your feet parallel and knees slightly bent.

2. With both hands, reach over your head and gently pull the back of your head forward and reach over your head and gently pull the back of your head forward and down.

3. Your chin should lower toward the middle of your clavicles (collarbones).

Benefit: Stretches neck muscles that tighten when you are paddling.

Triangle Pose

1. Stand with your legs 3 feet apart.

2. Keep the right foot pointing forward and turn the left foot sideways so your feet are perpendicular to each other.

3. Extend your arms out from the sides of your body at shoulder height. [1]

4. Bend your hip and waist to the left so the left hand contacts the lower portion of your left leg.

5. Turn your head toward the ceiling. [2]

6. Hold for 10 seconds to 1 minute before switching sides.

Benefit: Stretches and strengthens muscles at the hips and waist.

Reverse Triangle Pose

1. Stand with your legs 3 feet apart.

2. Keep the right foot pointing forward and turn the left foot sideways so your feet are perpendicular to each other.

3. Extend your arms out from the sides of your body at shoulder height.

4. Bend and rotate at the hip and waist to the left so your right hand contacts the lower portion of your left leg.

5. Turn your head toward the ceiling.

6. Hold for 10 seconds to 1 minute before switching sides.

Benefit: Stretches and strengthens muscles at the hips, waist, and lower back.

Advanced Shoulder Stretch

stretches

1. Bring your right hand behind your back so the fingers reach up between the shoulder blades.

2. Bring your left hand behind your head and neck so the fingers point down toward the opposite hand.

3. Bring both hands together so the fingers grip one another.

4. Hold for 10 seconds to 1 minute before switching sides.

Benefit: Stretches shoulder muscles and increases range of movement.
Note: You can grip a towel or leash cord with both hands if you're not able to get your hands close enough together for grasping fingers.
This exercise can be performed standing, seated, or kneeling.

Warrior Pose

1. Stand with your legs 3 three feet apart.

2. Keep your right foot pointing forward and turn your left foot sideways so your feet are perpendicular to each other.

3. Extend your arms out from the sides of your body at shoulder height.

4. Bend your left knee while your right leg remains straight as you shift your body's weight sideways to the left. Turn your head to the left.

5. Hold for 10 seconds to 1 minute before switching sides.

Benefit: Stretches inner thigh and strengthens leg and core muscles.

Side Reach

1. Stand with your legs 3 feet apart.

2. Keep the right foot pointing forward and turn the left foot sideways so your feet are perpendicular to each other.

3. Extend your arms out from the sides of your body at shoulder height.

4. Bend your left knee while your right leg remains straight as you shift your body's weight sideways to the left.

5. Lower your left hand to contact the left ankle as you reach up and over your head with your right arm.

6. Hold for 10 seconds to 1 minute before switching sides.

Benefit: Stretches torso muscles while strengthening leg muscles.

Upper Spinal Floor Twist

1. Lie on one side, with your knees pulled up into right angles with your hips and ankles.

2. Extend your arms in front of your body, with palms together. [1]

3. Exhale as you reach over your body with the upper arm and down to the floor on the opposite side. [2]

4. Keep your legs firmly anchored to the floor so the rotation occurs in the spine and torso.

5. Hold for 10 seconds to 1 minute.

6. Repeat on the opposite side.

Benefit: Promotes proper spinal rotation and torso flexibility.

Upward-Facing Dog

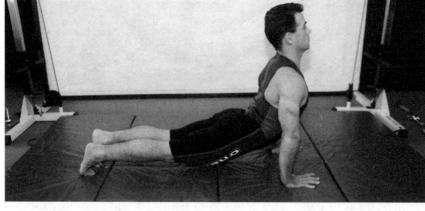

1. Begin in a push-up position, with arms and legs supporting your straight body above the floor.

2. Inhale as you bend your arms and lower your body toward the floor—but don't touch the floor.

3. Exhale as your chest pulls forward and upward and your arms press into a straightened position.

4. Perform at least 2 sets of 2 to 10 repetitions.

Benefit: Promotes spinal flexibility and upper body strength.

Downward-Facing Dog

1. Start on your hands and knees. Your hands should be below the shoulders and your knees should be below your hips, with your toes curled up on the floor.

2. Push your body back onto your hands and feet, with legs, arms, and back straight.

3. Press your heels to the floor while maintaining straight legs and push your hips away from your hands.

Benefit: Stretches lower back, hamstrings, and calf muscles that tighten when surfing.

Quadriceps Stretch

1. Stand on your right leg. For assistance with balance you can place your right hand against a wall.

2. Bend your left leg at the knee and grasp the roof of the foot with your left hand.

3. Keep both knees parallel, and tuck the buttocks downward.

4. Repeat with the opposite leg.

Benefit: Reduces hip tension for better balance.

Chapter 3

Sun Salutation

The Sun Salutation is a series of gentle, flowing yoga poses that are often performed as a morning wake-up routine. The Sun Salutation can also be performed as a warm-up routine prior to surfing. This series of movements enhances flexibility of the spine and legs and chest while strengthening the arms and shoulders and enhancing the body's sense of balance and coordination.

Try to hold each pose for 5 to 15 seconds before transitioning to the next pose in the sequence. Perform the series of 12 poses three to four times. When performing the repetition of the lunge position, be sure to alternate legs. A single sequence of the 12 poses usually takes about one minute.

Concentrate to maintain an awareness of your breath while entering and exiting each pose. When breathing, be sure to inhale into the diaphragm, filling the midsection as deeply as possible.

Prayer Pose

yoga warm-up

1. Stand tall with your feet at hip width.

2. Gently press your palms together in a prayer position.

3. Inhale deeply.

Mountain Pose

1. Exhale as you reach upward with both arms.

Forward Bend

1. Inhale as you bend your body forward.

2. Lower your torso, with arms reaching forward.

3. Bring your hands to the floor as the back bends slightly.

Lunge Position

1. Bend both knees, with hands flat on the floor.

2. Exhale as you step back with your right foot until the left knee is at a right angle.

3. Allow your midsection to rest against the top of your left thigh.

Plank Position

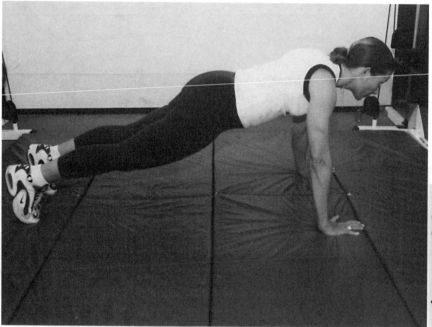

1. Bring your left leg back parallel to the right leg.

2. Inhale as you keep your arms straight to support the body's weight.

3. Keep torso and legs straight so the body resembles a plank.

Grasshopper Pose

1. From the plank position, bend at the elbows and knees.

2. Exhale as you allow your body to lower until your chest almost scrapes the floor.

Upward-Facing Dog

1. Inhale as you press your chest upward and forward as your arms and legs straighten.

2. Keep the thigh muscles contracted to help support your body.

Downward-Facing Dog

1. Exhale as you push your body backward onto your hands and feet as the legs, arms, and back straighten.

2. Press your heels to the floor while maintaining straight legs and push the hips away from the hands.

3. Point the sit bones at the base of the buttocks toward the ceiling.

Lunge Position

1. Bend both knees, with hands flat on the floor.

2. Inhale as you step forward with the right foot until the right knee is at a right angle.

3. Allow the midsection to rest against the top of the right thigh.

Deep Forward Bend

1. Bring your left foot forward to be parallel with the right foot.

2. Exhale as you bend your body forward.

3. Inhale as you raise your torso, with arms parallel with the spine.

Mountain Pose

1. Exhale as you reach upward with both arms.

Prayer Pose

1. Stand tall with feet together as you lower your arms.

2. Gently press your palms together in a prayer position.

3. Inhale deeply.

4. Repeat entire sequence of poses.

Chapter 4

Strength Training

Bursts of speed are often required when surfing. This is why strength training is a powerful component in your conditioning program. As mentioned earlier, strength training consists of relatively short bursts of muscular force anywhere up to 1 or 2 minutes. This type of training builds size and strength in the muscles and conditions them to store more energy for immediate use.

However, after only twenty or thirty seconds of such activity the source of immediate energy is exhausted and the muscles (and your liver) have to release a form of sugar that is broken down to create even more energy. Strength training conditions the body to store more of this sugar for future needs. This chemical reaction not only allows the muscles to continue generating force but also unfortunately creates lactic acid. Lactic acid accumulation in muscle tissue creates a burning sensation in the muscles. This burning may cause you to stop before you want. Strength training increases your tolerance for lactic acid, allowing you to paddle harder and farther. Other benefits of strength training include:

- Increased energy levels.
- Reduced injury potential.
- Increased bone density.

- Increased body circulation.

- Heightened body awareness.

When performing strength exercises, remember the five Rs, important elements of every strength program:

1. Resistance: The amount of weight or other resistance used during an exercise. Whatever the amount of resistance chosen, it's essential to retain proper form while doing the exercise.

2. Repetitions: The number of times a movement is performed during a set of an exercise. Typically, the lower the number of repetitions (with high resistance), the more basic strength is trained; the higher the repetitions (with low resistance), the more muscular endurance is trained.

3. Range of motion: The movement a muscle is responsible for. Ideally, it is best to train the muscle's fullest range of motion.

4. Rest: The amount of time spent resting between each set of exercises. An ideal rest period is between 30 seconds and 2 minutes, but the rest period may increase with greater intensity of exercise.

5. Recovery: The amount of time spent between strength training workouts of the same muscle group. It is often recommended that you allow 48 hours after strength training one muscle group before exercising that same group again, though this is not an ironclad rule. If you find that you are strength training the same muscle groups two days in a row, it would be wise to change the selection of exercises for the following day (for example, when exercising the chest [pectorals], perform the dumbbell bench press on Monday and perform stability ball push-ups on Tuesday).

When you are training for strength, try to achieve temporary muscle fatigue in one set of each exercise. Temporary muscle fatigue occurs when the muscles are so exhausted that another repetition cannot be performed with proper technique.

In selecting your strength workout program, choose a range of exercises in order to incorporate all the major muscle groups. If you intend to perform strength workouts more than three to four times per week, it may be better to focus on upper body on one day and lower body on a different day.

It's important to maintain proper form from start to finish in a set. It's equally important to have someone act as a spotter for safety when you perform exercises with weights that are suspended above your body. If you experience pain during an exercise, stop immediately and omit that exercise from the workout for the time being.

Exhale during the exertion phase of each exercise (for example, exhaling as you push upward during the dumbbell bench press). If you experience dizziness or pain during an exercise, stop immediately and omit that exercise from the workout for the time being.

Some of the following exercises require a workout facility with ample equipment and space to execute the drills safely, but other exercises can be performed at home. Therefore, even if you're not a member of a gym, you can still create an effective program of strength training. The workout programs in chapter 9 list suggested schedules and provide the appropriate number of sets and repetitions for the exercises.

The exercises illustrated in this chapter are divided into three categories: upper body, lower body, and torso. Each description lists the muscles that are involved in the exercise, and these muscles are shown in the Muscle Chart in appendix 4.

Upper Body Exercises

Push-up on the Knees

1. Place your hands in a parallel position just out-side shoulder width.

2. Support your body on hands and knees.

3. Inhale as you lower your body until your chest barely touches the floor, or until the elbows form a 90-degree an-gle. [1]

4. Exhale when pushing up. [2]

5. Keep your body rigid by contracting the abdominal muscles.

6. Do not allow your back to arch or bow at any time.

Muscles involved: Pectorals, deltoids, triceps.

Benefit: Strengthens upper body for pop-ups (pushing up on a surf-board to get up on your feet).

Note: This is a good way for a beginner to perform this exercise.

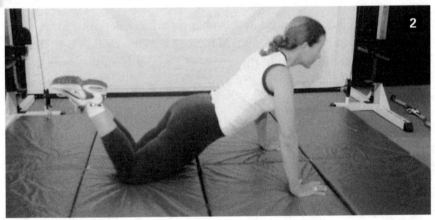

Push-Up on the Toes

1. Place your hands in a parallel position just outside shoulder width.

2. Support your body on hands and toes.

3. Inhale as you lower your body until your chest barely touches the floor, or until the elbows form a 90-degree angle. [1]

4. Exhale when pushing up. [2]

5. Keep your body rigid by contracting the abdominal muscles.

6. Do not allow your back to arch or bow at any time.

Muscles involved: Pectorals, deltoids, triceps.
Benefit: Strengthens upper body for pop-ups.
Note: This position is more demanding than push-ups on the knees.

Push-Up on Balance Board

1. Place your hands in a parallel position on the balance board, just outside shoulder width.

2. Support your body on hands and toes.

3. Inhale as you lower your body until your chest barely touches the balance board, or until the elbows form a 90-degree angle. [1]

4. Exhale when pushing up. [2]

5. Keep your body rigid by contracting the abdominal muscles.

6. Do not allow your back to arch or bow at any time.

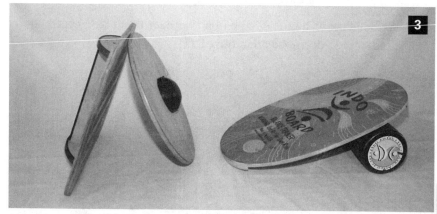

Muscles involved: Pectorals, deltoids, triceps.

Benefit: Enhances coordination for pop-ups.

Note: When you first use a balance board for push-ups, it may be best to start with push-ups on the knees.

The balance board is designed to wobble from side to side, producing an effect similar to popping up on a surfboard (pushing off a board to get up on your feet). Its use trains the body to be more balanced when exerting force. There are many types of balance boards, such as those shown in the accompanying photo [3]. The board pictured with the exercises is a piece of 20-inch by 20-inch plywood with two semicircular pieces of wood screwed into the bottom. You can either buy or make your own balance board.

Plyometric Push-Up on Balance Board

1. Begin with your hands on the balance board.

2. Perform a push-up quickly, so that your body is pushed into the air and your hands are freed.

3. Quickly lift your hands off the board and let them land on the floor on either side of the balance board. [1]

4. Perform another quick push-up so your body is again airborne. [2]

5. Let your hands return back on to the balance board. [3]

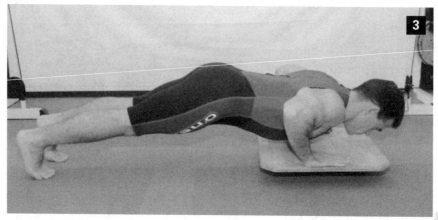

Muscles involved: Pectorals, deltoids, triceps.

Benefit: Trains upper body to be quick and explosive.

Note: This is one of the more advanced ways to perform a push-up. This exercise will train the muscles to respond quickly and powerfully to propel the body off the floor. It's a good idea to first perform this exercise on the knees before advancing to the toe position.

Bench Press

1. Lie on your back on a bench, with your feet flat.

2. Grip a barbell with hands placed at just outside shoulder width.

3. Support the barbell with straight arms, above the shoulders.

4. Inhale as you lower the barbell to a point above the middle of your chest (elbows should be at right angles). [1]

5. Exhale as you press the weight upward to the starting position. [2]

Muscles involved: Pectorals, deltoids, triceps.
Benefit: Helps balance strength of upper body.
Note: This exercise also can be performed with a dumbbell in each hand, instead of the barbell.

Lat Pulldown

1. Get down on one knee, positioning the other foot forward, and grasp the bar. [1]

2. Exhale as you pull the bar down below your chin. [2]

3. Inhale as you return the bar to the starting position.

Muscles involved: Latissimus dorsi, middle trapezius, posterior deltoid, and biceps.

Benefit: Strengthens major paddling muscles.

Note: You can grip the bar in a number of ways: wide grip, narrow grip, and underhand grip. Each grip incorporates a large group of upper-body muscles, though the focus may be on one muscle more than another, depending on the grip. You can alternate between grips from one workout to the next.

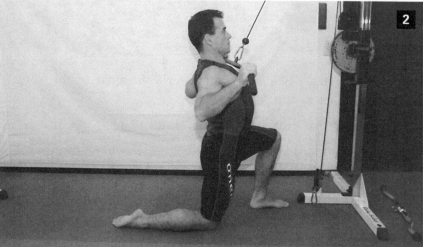

Bench Dip

1. Place both hands behind you, shoulder-width apart, on the front edge of a bench, chair, or box.

2. Put your feet up on another bench, chair, or box.

3. Push up, supporting your body weight on straightened arms.

4. Inhale as you bend your elbows and lower your body until elbows and shoulders are at the same height. [1]

5. Exhale as you push your body back up to the starting position. [2]

Muscles involved: Pectorals, deltoids, triceps.

Benefit: Strengthens paddling muscles.

Note: When first doing this exercise, start by performing it with your feet on the floor, rather than up on another bench, chair, or box.

Pull-Up

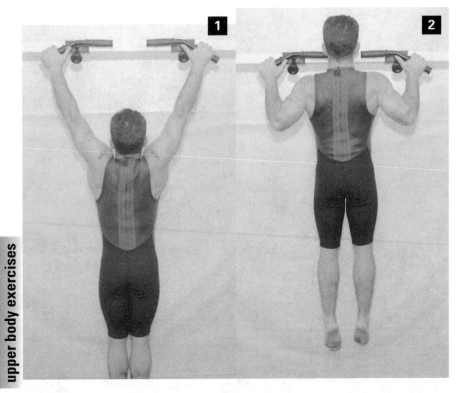

1. Grasp a pull-up bar, with your hands shoulder-width apart. Start from a straight-arm hanging position. [1]

2. Exhale as you pull your body up, so your chin is raised above the bar. [2]

3. Inhale as you lower your body back to the starting position.

4. Do not kick with your legs to help raise your body.

Muscles involved: Latissimus dorsi, middle trapezius, posterior deltoid, biceps.

Benefit: Strengthens major paddling muscles.

Straight-Arm Pulldown

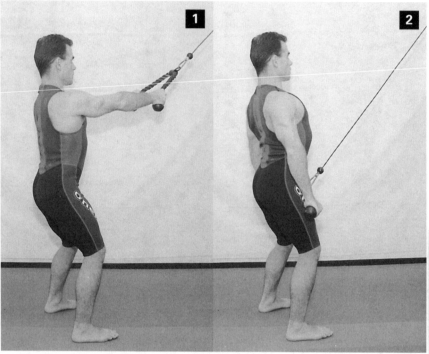

1. Stand upright, with your feet parallel and knees slightly bent.

2. Grab the handles of the lat pulldown machine (also called a high pulley cable station) with hands shoulder-width apart, elbows straight, and arms stiff. [1]

3. Exhale as you pull the bar downward to the front of your thighs. [2]

4. Inhale as you return the bar to shoulder height; your arms should be parallel to the floor.

Muscles involved: Latissimus dorsi, pectorals, posterior deltoid, triceps.
Benefit: Strengthens body for double-arm paddle.

Horizontal Pull-Up

1. Grasp a bar with your hands shoulder-width apart and your feet on the floor in front of your body.

2. Keep both knees slightly bent. [1]

3. Keeping your body stiff and straight, exhale as you pull your chest up to the bar. [2]

4. Inhale as you lower your body back to the starting position.

5. Keep the abdominal muscles tight to prevent your back from arching or your hips from sagging.

Muscles involved: Middle trapezius, rhomboids, posterior deltoid, biceps.

Benefit: Strengthens midback paddling muscles.

Single Straight-Arm Pulldown

1. Bend your legs slightly, keeping your abdominals firm.

2. Keep your torso still.

3. Grip a handle on the upper pulley of the cable station in your right hand. [1]

4. Exhale as you pull the handle down to your right thigh. [2]

5. Inhale as you return your arm to the starting position.

6. Repeat, gripping with your left hand.

Muscles involved: Pectorals, latissimus dorsi, triceps brachii, serratus anterior, abdominals.

Benefit: Helps establish more balance with left and right arms.

Dumbbell Pullover

1. Lie on your back on a bench, with both feet firmly planted on the bench.

2. Grip a dumbbell with both hands, with your arms straight above your head, the arms slightly bent but stiff. [1]

3. Inhale as you lower the dumbbell over your head and toward the floor, until the dumbbell reaches head height. [2]

4. Exhale as you reverse direction and raise the dumbbell back to the starting position.

5. Keep your abdominal muscles contracted to protect the lower back.

Muscles involved: Pectorals, latissimus dorsi, posterior deltoid, triceps.
Benefit: Strengthens paddling muscles.

upper body exercises

One-Arm Row

1. Place your left knee and left hand on a bench.

2. Position your right leg on the floor, with the knee slightly bent, while your right hand grasps a dumbbell. [1]

3. Keep your back straight and your head in a neutral position.

4. Exhale as you lift the dumbbell up to your rib cage. [2]

5. Inhale as you lower the dumbbell back to a straight-arm position.

6. Change sides and repeat.

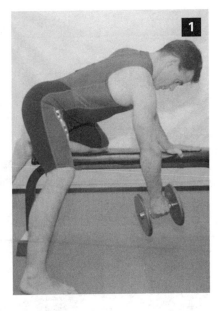

Muscles involved: Latissimus dorsi, middle trapezius, rhomboids, posterior deltoid, biceps.

Benefit: Strengthens midback for paddling.

Reverse Dumbbell Fly

1. Place your feet parallel and hip-width apart.

2. Bend at the waist so your shoulders are slightly above hip height; keep your back straight.

3. Grasp a dumbbell in each hand. [1]

4. Exhale as you raise the dumbbells upward and out from the body until the dumbbells are shoulder height. [2]

5. Inhale as you lower the dumbbells back to the starting position.

6. Keep your torso as still as possible.

7. Do not allow your lower back to lift the torso as the dumbbells are raised.

Muscles involved: Middle trapezius, rhomboids, posterior deltoid.
Benefit: Promotes shoulder stabilization.

Bent-Over Row

1. In a standing position, grasp a barbell with a shoulder-width grip.

2. Keeping your back straight, bend at the hips and knees until your torso is almost parallel to the floor.

3. The barbell should hang directly below your shoulders. [1]

4. Exhale as you pull the barbell to the center of your chest. [2]

5. Inhale as you return the barbell to the starting position.

6. Do not lift with the lower back muscles; those muscles should be contracting but not lifting.

Muscles involved: Rhomboids, middle trapezius, latissimus dorsi, posterior deltoid, biceps brachii.

Benefit: Builds strength for supporting torso above surfboard.

Triceps Pushdown

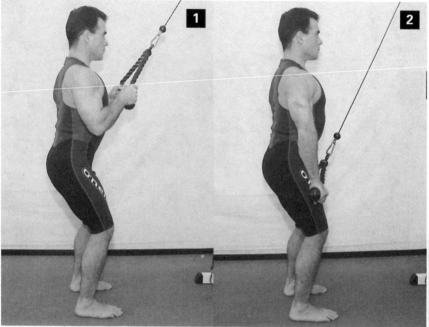

1. Stand upright, with your feet hip-width apart and knees slightly bent.

2. Grasp the handle of the upper pulley on the cable station or two ends of a rope handle with both hands and pull down so your elbows are nestled beside your rib cage. This is the starting position. [1]

3. Exhale as you push down to a straight-arm position. [2]

4. Inhale as you bend your elbows and return to the starting position.

5. Keep your elbows beside the rib cage at all times so the movement rotates only through the elbows.

Muscles involved: Triceps.
Benefit: Builds strong paddling arms.

External Rotation I

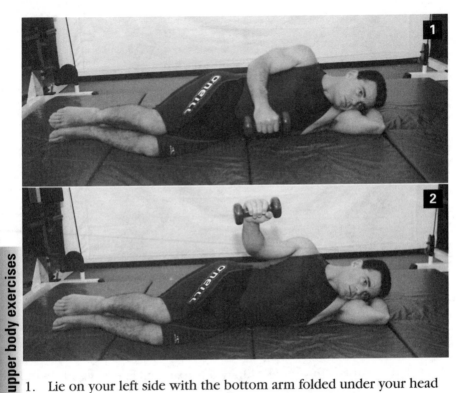

1. Lie on your left side with the bottom arm folded under your head for support and your legs slightly bent and parallel.

2. Bend the upper arm at a right angle, with the elbow pressed into your rib cage. [1]

3. Hold a dumbbell in that hand and exhale as you lift the dumbbell above the elbow. [2]

4. Inhale as you lower the dumbbell back to the starting position.

5. Repeat on the other side.

Muscles involved: Rotator cuff muscles.
Benefit: Promotes shoulder stabilization.

External Rotation II

1. Stand with your feet parallel and hip-width apart.

2. With a dumbbell in your left hand, raise that elbow up to shoulder height out away from your body, with the dumbbell hanging down. Keep the elbow bent at a right angle (90 degrees); keep the upper arm at a right angle from the midline of your body. [1]

3. Keeping the elbow at shoulder height, exhale as you raise the dumbbell up directly above the elbow. [2]

4. Inhale as you lower the dumbbell back to the starting position.

5. Repeat, with the dumbbell in your right hand.

Muscles involved: Rotator cuff muscles.
Benefit: Encourages shoulder function and stabilization.

Lower Body Exercises

Squat

1. Stand with feet hip-width apart or slightly wider.

2. Rest a barbell on your shoulders, just above the shoulder blades (not on your neck). [1]

3. Inhale as your body descends.

4. Allow your hips and knees to bend; keep your chest upright. [2]

5. Reverse direction and exhale until your legs are almost straight.

6. Be sure your hips and shoulders lower and raise at the same time.

7. Do not allow your hips to descend below the knees.

Muscles involved: Gluteals, hamstrings, quadriceps.
Benefit: Enhances leg strength and balance.
Note: Instead of the barbell on your shoulders, you can do this exercise with dumbbells held by your hips, or with body weight alone with no weights.

lower body exercises

Split Squat

1. Stand in a forward split position with your feet pointing straight ahead, the right foot 2 to 3 feet ahead of the left foot.

2. Rest a barbell on your shoulders, just above the shoulder blades (not on the neck). [1]

3. Inhale as your body descends until the rear knee is an inch from the floor. [2]

4. Reverse direction and exhale until your legs are almost straight.

5. Be sure your hips and shoulders lower and raise at the same time.

6. Repeat, with your left leg forward.

Muscles involved: Gluteals, hamstrings, and quadriceps.
Benefit: Builds leg strength and balance.
Note: Instead of the barbell on your shoulders, you can do this exercise with dumbbells held by your hips, or with body weight alone with no weights.

Forward Lunge

1. Stand upright, holding dumbbells or placing hands by your hips.

2. Inhale as you take a step forward with your right foot. [1]

3. Descend until your hips and forward knee are at the same height. [2]

4. Exhale as you push off the floor with your right leg and return to the starting position.

5. Keep the upper body upright at all times; do not allow your shoulders to push back first.

6. The movement should originate in the hips and not the lower back.

7. Repeat, stepping forward with your left foot.

lower body exercises

Muscles involved: Gluteals, hamstrings, quadriceps.

Benefit: Builds leg strength and balance with change of direction.

Note: Instead of the dumbbells by your hips, you can do this exercise with a barbell resting on top of your shoulder blades (not on the neck), or with body weight alone with no weights.

The difference between a lunge and a squat is that the squat employs a straight up-and-down movement whereas the lunge combines a forward-and-back movement combined with the up-and-down movement.

Reverse Lunge

1. Stand upright feet parallel and hip-width apart, with a barbell resting on your shoulders, on top of the shoulder blades (not on the neck).

2. Inhale as you take a step backward with your left foot. [1]

3. Descend until your hips and forward knee are at the same height. [2]

4. Exhale as you push off the floor with your left leg and return to the starting position.

5. Keep your upper body upright, both on the descent and on the return; do not allow the shoulders to push forward first.

6. The movement should originate in the hips and not the lower back.

7. Repeat, stepping backward with your right foot.

Muscles involved: Gluteals, hamstrings, quadriceps.
Benefit: Builds leg strength and balance with change of direction.
Note: Instead of the barbell on your shoulders, you can do this exercise with dumbbells held by your hips, or with body weight alone with no weights.

Walking Lunge

1. Stand upright, holding dumbbells or placing hands by your hips.
2. Inhale as you take a step forward with your left foot and your body descends until the hips and forward knee are at the same height. [1]
3. Exhale as your forward leg pulls and the rear leg pushes your body forward to a standing position. [2]
4. Repeat, stepping forward with your right foot.
5. Keep the upper body upright at all times; do not allow the shoulders to push forward first.
7. The movement should originate in the hips and not the lower back.

Muscles involved: Gluteals, hamstrings, quadriceps.
Benefit: Builds leg strength, balance, and coordination.
Note: Instead of the dumbbells by your hips, you can do this exercise with a barbell resting on top of your shoulder blades (not on the neck), or with body weight alone with no weights.

Wall Sit

1. Get into a sitting position against a wall so your lower back is flat and your knees and hips are the same height from the floor—as if sitting in a chair.

2. Your feet should be 4 inches apart, pointing straight ahead and parallel.

3. Your feet should be away from the wall so the heels are directly below the knees.

4. Ankles, knees, and hips should all be at right angles.

5. The weight of your body should be pressed through the heels and not the toes.

6. Hold for about 30 seconds.

Muscles involved: Rectus femoris.
Benefit: Enhances leg strength and reduces lower back tension.

The Chop

1. Stand with your legs 3 feet apart, in a slight squat position.

2. With both hands, grab the handle of the upper pulley on the cable station. [1]

3. Keep your arms rigid but slightly bent at the elbow.

4. Exhale as you twist your waist and pull downward with both arms, to the left side of your body. [2]

5. Inhale as you twist your body back to the starting position.

6. Repeat, pulling downward to the right side.

7. Keep your arms in front of your torso as the body twists during the exercise.

Muscles involved: External and internal obliques, latissimus dorsi.
Benefit: Strengthens rotational muscles of the torso.

Abdominal Crunch

1. Lie on your back, with knees bent at right angles and feet flat.

2. Clasp your hands together and cradle the back of your head. [1]

3. Keep your shoulder blades contracted so your elbows stay parallel with your shoulders.

4. Exhale as you lift your head, elbows, and shoulders off the floor. [2]

5. As you lift, keep your lower back pressed into the floor and your abdominal muscles contracted.

5. Inhale as you lower yourself back to the floor.

Muscles involved: Abdominals.

Benefit: Strengthens torso and stretches lower back.

Note: For added intensity, perform the same exercise with your legs raised off the floor—point your legs directly upward so your toes are directly above the hips.

torso exercises

Twisting Lift

1. Stand with your legs 3 feet apart, in a slight squat position.

2. With both hands, grab the handle of the lower pulley of the cable station.

3. Keep your arms rigid but slightly bent at the elbow. [1]

4. Exhale as you twist your waist and pull upward with both arms, to the right side of your body. [2]

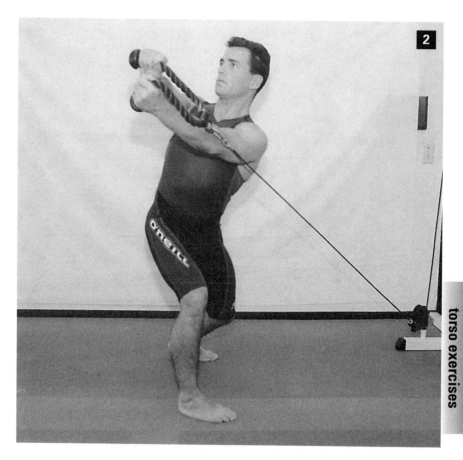

5. Inhale as you twist your body back to the starting position.

6. Repeat, pulling upward to the left side.

7. Keep your arms in front of your torso as the body twists during the exercise.

Muscles involved: External and internal obliques, latissimus dorsi.
Benefit: Strengthens rotational muscles of the torso.

Oblique Crunch

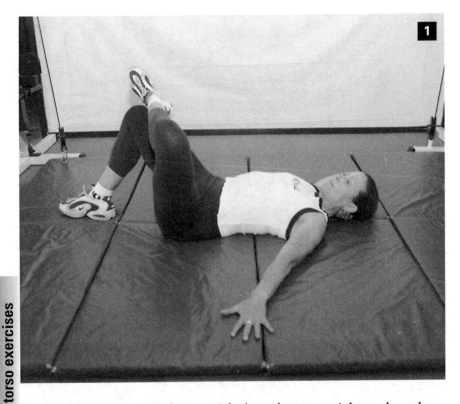

1. Lie on your back, with your right knee bent at a right angle and foot flat.

2. Cross your left ankle over the bent knee.

3. With your right hand, cradle the back of your head; place your left arm, palm down, away from your body. [1]

4. Exhale as you lift your right arm off the floor, along with your head and right shoulder, in the direction of the crossed leg. [2]

5. Inhale as you lower yourself back to the floor.

6. Keep your hips and legs as still as possible.

7. Repeat, using the opposite side.

Muscles involved: Abdominals and obliques.
Benefit: Strengthens torso rotation and stretches lower back.

Opposite Arm and Leg Raise

1. Lie face-down with arms outstretched and legs straight.

2. Exhale as you lift your right arm and your left leg off the floor. [1]

3. Inhale as you lower the arm and leg back to the floor.

4. Repeat, using the left arm and right leg. [2]

5. Keep your head facing the floor through the entire exercise.

Muscles involved: Gluteals, lower trapezius, spinal erectors.
Benefit: Conditions body to strengthen it in a face-down position.

Lateral Torso Lift

1. Lie on your left side with both legs together and the lower elbow propped under your shoulder. [1]

2. Exhale as you lift your hips off the floor until just the left foot remains on the floor; the leg should not touch the ground. [2]

3. Inhale as you lower your body back to the starting position.

4. Repeat, lying on your right side.

Muscles involved: Internal and external obliques.
Benefit: Strengthens the sides of the torso.

Bicycles

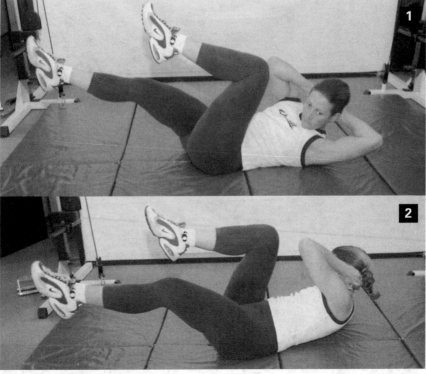

1. Lie on your back with hands clasped behind your head and elbows out away from your body.

2. Exhale as you pull up so that the right elbow touches the left knee. [1]

3. Repeat using the left elbow and the right knee. [2]

Muscles involved: Internal and external obliques, psoas major, abdominals.

Benefit: Strengths core muscles responsible for rotation.

Chapter 5

Medicine Balls and Stability Balls

Medicine Ball Training

Looking back at the history of fitness in America, it's hard not to laugh at some of the contraptions purported to be beneficial to good health—from the waist belt connected to a vibrating machine that was supposed to jiggle away unwanted pounds to the little electric shock pads that would jolt a beer belly into the abdomen of Adonis.

At least one fitness item, however, has stood the test of time and is now receiving new attention: the good old medicine ball. A medicine ball is simply a heavy ball used in performing various bending, throwing, lifting, and twisting movements. These movements mimic the torso action involved when riding a wave. It would be dangerous to play catch with a dumbbell but it can be a lot of fun with a medicine ball. Medicine balls come in all sizes and weights, from one pound to 25 pounds, and are stuffed with rags and sand to provide weight. They can be purchased at most sporting goods stores. It might be wise to start with a 3-pound to 5-pound ball to help train the muscles in the proper movement before increasing intensity with heavier balls.

Medicine ball movements require cooperation and coordination between the body's core muscles in the torso with those of the arms and legs. Medicine ball exercises are more functional and specific to everyday life because they focus on transferring force from the core to the rest of the body. Many of today's exercise machines fail to do this because they concentrate on isolating movements rather than on those that are more complex.

The following medicine ball exercises are great for surfers. Consider medicine ball exercises as another portion of the strength training part of your program. Exercises with a medicine ball are also a great way to warm up *all* the body's muscles.

Seated Twist

1. Sit with your legs in front of your body, and your knees slightly bent so your heels dig into the floor.

2. Holding onto the medicine ball with both hands, swing the ball to the left side of your body. [1]

3. Reverse direction to the other side. [2]

4. Keep your arms straight in front of your chest, as if frozen in that position, so that rotation occurs at the waist and not at the shoulders.

5. Make certain your head rotates with your torso.

Benefit: Strengthens torso rotation.

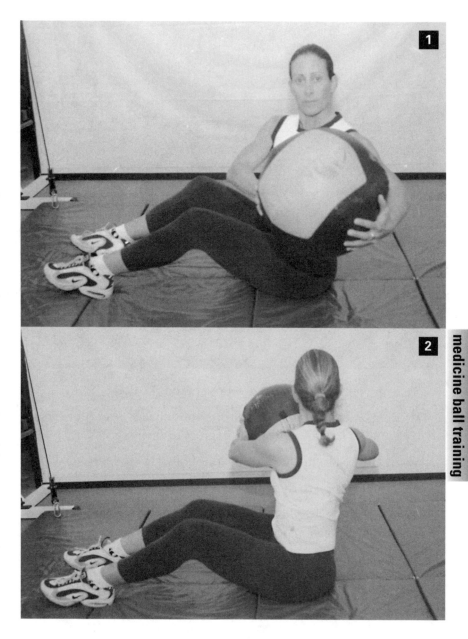

Medicine Balls and Stability Balls **101**

Russian Twist

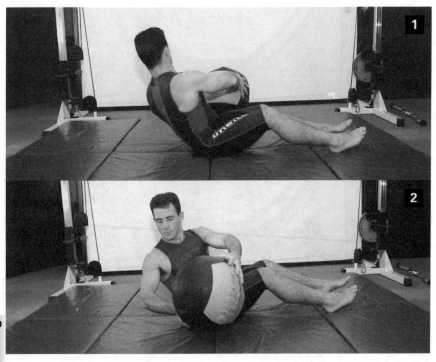

1. Sit with your knees bent and your heels on the floor.

2. Holding on to the medicine ball with both hands, lean your torso back until it is at an angle of 45 degrees to the floor.

3. Swing the ball to the left side of your body. [1]

4. Reverse direction to the other side. [2]

5. Keep your arms straight in front of your chest, as if frozen in that position, so that rotation occurs at the waist and not at the shoulders.

6. Make certain your head also rotates with your torso.

Benefit: Strengthens torso rotation while engaging hip and abdominal muscles.

Overhead Toss

1. Lie on your back with knees bent at right angles.

2. With both hands over your head, grip the medicine ball. [1]

3. Exhale as you curl your body upward and hurl the ball forward. [2]

4. Inhale as you catch the ball when it is thrown back to you and as you lower back to the starting position.

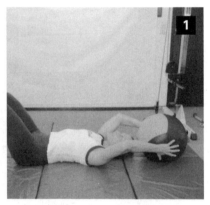

Benefit: Strengthens abdominals and torso flexion.

Note: You'll need a partner to catch and return the ball. Also, a trampoline-like device is available that is angled to bounce the ball back to the thrower.

medicine ball training

Rotary Torso Toss

1. In an upright kneeling position, grip the medicine ball with both hands.

2. Begin with the medicine ball on one side of your body. [1]

3. Exhale as you twist your body in order to toss the ball to the opposite side. [2]

4. Inhale as you catch the ball when it is thrown back to you and as you swing back to the starting position.

Benefit: Strengthens rotational movement and the body's ability to transfer force from the torso to the upper and lower body.
Note: You'll need a partner to catch and return the ball.

Chest Pass Crunch

1. Lie on your back with knees bent at right angles.

2. With both hands above your chest, grip the medicine ball. [1]

3. Exhale as you curl your body upward and hurl the ball forward. [2]

4. Inhale as you catch the ball when it is thrown back to you and as you lower back to the starting position.

Benefit: Strengthens abdominals, upper body, and torso flexion.
Note: You'll need a partner to catch and return the ball. Also, a trampoline-like device is available that is angled to bounce the ball back to the thrower.

medicine ball training

Stability Ball Training

Stability balls are inflatable rubber balls that resemble the old "hippity-hoppity" toys we bounced around on as children. The main difference is that the stability ball does not have a handle. Stability balls come in different sizes, from 2 feet in diameter on up.

The purpose of exercising with these balls is to enhance the body's balance, core strength, and ability to maintain stability. When exercising on an unstable surface, the muscle groups or muscles that provide stability (the rotator cuff, abdominals, and lower back) become more active.

The more stable the body, the less likely an injury. A crude analogy of the difference between weak and strong stabilizing muscles would be a house kept together with staples compared to one held with six-inch nails. Many traditional strength training exercises (e.g. bench press, bicep curls) do not address the stabilizing muscles. The exercise merely demands sheer force from the body any way it can be created. Therefore it is essential that other exercises be incorporated to address the stabilizing muscles.

Some of these stability ball exercises may appear gentle in comparison to other strength exercises (e.g. squats, lunges) but they nevertheless focus on strengthening muscles and should be considered part of your strength training program. Many of the targeted muscles are small and do not demand tremendous amounts of work. Nor will these exercises make you out of breath. Nevertheless, these stability ball exercises are extremely important in maintaining proper stability.

The exercises illustrated here will introduce you to the stability ball and serve as a reference once you've started your training program. When performing the exercises, be sure to have ample space free of sharp or hard objects in case you lose your balance.

Abdominal Crunch

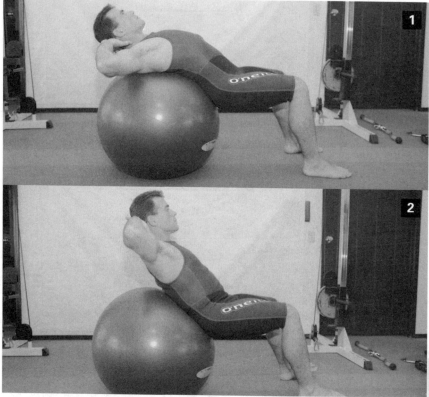

1. Lie on your back on the stability ball, with your feet placed on a wall or flat on the floor.

2. Cradle your head with both hands, with shoulder blades pinched together. [1]

3. Exhale as you curl your torso upward; your spine should be at 30 degrees of flexion; the lower back should not lift off the floor. [2]

4. Inhale as you lower your torso back to the starting position.

Benefit: Strengthens abdominals while maintaining balance.

Trunk (Torso) Rotation

1. Begin with shoulders, neck, and the back of the head resting on top of the stability ball, with hips, thighs, and spine parallel to the floor and also supported by your feet on the floor.

2. Clasp your hands together, with arms straight above your chest. [1]

3. Exhale as you twist your torso to the left until your left arm becomes parallel to the floor.

4. Inhale as you twist your torso back to the starting position.

5. Exhale as you repeat the movement to the right. [2]

6. Inhale as you twist your torso back to the starting position.

Benefit: Strengthens rotational muscles while promoting balance.

Push-Up

1. Lie face down on the stability ball and place both hands forward on the floor.

2. Keep your body rigid as your hands walk forward until the thighs are on top of the ball and the torso is supported with the arms. The ball should end up between your knees and ankles.

3. Inhale as you lower your body until the chest is an inch off the floor. [1]

4. Exhale as you press your body upward to the starting position. [2]

Benefit: Strengthens upper body and rotator cuff while increasing stability of the torso.

Note: To increase exercise intensity, walk your body out so only your feet are on top of the ball when performing the push upward.

Back Extension

1. Lie stomach down on the stability ball, with your feet anchored against a wall.

2. Place your hands behind your head, with elbows out. [1]

3. Exhale as you raise your body to a straight position; do not arch your back. Press down your body's weight to keep the ball from moving. [2]

4. Inhale as you lower your body back to the starting position.

Benefit: Strengthens lower back and buttocks while maintaining balance.

stability ball training

Back Extension with Twist

1. Lie stomach down on the stability ball, with your feet anchored against a wall.

2. Place your hands behind your head, with elbows out.

3. Exhale as you raise and twist your body to a position where one shoulder is higher than the other; do not arch your back. [1]

4. Inhale as you lower your body back to the starting position.

5. Repeat, raising the opposite shoulder. [2]

Benefit: Strengthens lower back rotation while maintaining balance.

stability ball training

Chapter 6

Skill Transfer Exercises

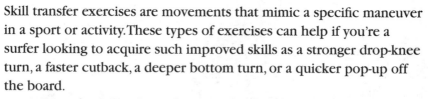

Skill transfer exercises are movements that mimic a specific maneuver in a sport or activity. These types of exercises can help if you're a surfer looking to acquire such improved skills as a stronger drop-knee turn, a faster cutback, a deeper bottom turn, or a quicker pop-up off the board.

Among the following exercises, select the ones that will help condition you for the maneuver you want to focus on, and add them to your fitness program.

Reverse Lunge

for a stronger drop-knee turn

1. Stand upright (feet hip-width apart and parallel), with a barbell resting on your shoulders, on top of the shoulder blades (not on the neck).

2. Inhale as you take a step backward with your left foot. [1]

3. Descend until your hips and forward knee are at the same height. [2]

4. Exhale as you push off the floor with your left leg and return to the starting position.

surf skills

114 *Skill Transfer Exercises*

5. Keep your upper body upright, both on the descent and on the return; do not allow the shoulders to push forward first.

6. The movement should originate in the hips and not the lower back.

7. Repeat, stepping backward with your right foot.

Muscles involved: Gluteals, hamstrings, quadriceps.
Note: Instead of the barbell on your shoulders, you can do this exercise with dumbbells held by your hips, or with body weight alone with no weights.

Hanging Leg Lift

for off the top

1. With your upper arms placed in straps, hang from a chin-up bar, or grasp the bar as if about to perform a pull-up. [1]

2. Exhale as you bend both legs and lift your feet up and to the side. [2]

3. Your feet should be raised to the same height as your hips.

4. Inhale as you lower your legs to the starting position.

5. Be sure to alternate raises from left to right.

Muscles involved: Psoas major, hip abductors, rectus abdominals.

Supine Eagles

for a deeper bottom turn

1. Lie supine (on your back), with your legs straight and arms away from the body, with palms down.

2. Exhale as you lift your left leg up and across your body until the toes touch your right hand. [1]

3. Inhale as you return the leg to the starting position.

4. Switch legs, bringing your right toes up to your left hand. [2]

5. Keep both shoulders in contact with the floor at all times.

Muscles involved: Psoas major, quadriceps, obliques.

surf skills

Standing Torso Rotation

for stronger cutbacks

1. Stand in a forward split position with your legs 2 to 3 feet apart.

2. Hold light dumbbells or medicine balls (with handles) in each hand.

3. Lower your body until your hips are at the same height as the front knee.

4. Raise your arms away from your body, to just below shoulder height.

5. Rotate through the hips as you swing your arms clockwise [1], and then counterclockwise back to the starting position [2].

6. Your entire body should rotate at the same time.

Muscles involved: Lower back, rectus abdominals, obliques.

surf skills

Burpees

for quicker pop-ups

1. Begin in the down phase of a push-up.

2. Place your hands directly below your shoulders, with your body lifted just off the floor. [1]

3. In one quick move, push up off the floor.

4. Bring both feet forward into a regular or goofy-foot surfboard stance. [2]

5. Quickly return to the starting position and repeat.

Muscles involved: Pectorals, deltoids, triceps, psoas major.

surf skills

Popping Push-Up

for stronger pop-ups

surf skills

1. Prepare to perform a push-up on the toes. [1]

2. Perform the push-up with enough explosive power that the hands lift off the floor. [2]

3. Lower the body, in a controlled manner, to the downward phase of the push-up.

4. Do not allow your body to lose its rigidity.

5. Do not let your hips or back sag at any time.

Muscles involved: Pectorals, deltoids, triceps.

Advanced Balance Training

The following exercises are devoted to balance and coordination. These are two key components of surfing that traditional strength and endurance training programs do not necessarily include. The average ride on a wave lasts less than 30 seconds. That is not a lot of time to develop balance skills. If you are a beginning surfer, your ride will last only a few seconds. If you are a seasoned surfer, your surfing is limited to when there are waves. Wouldn't it be nice to be able to spend more time developing balance and coordination? This is where the Indo Board can make a big difference. This tool is basically an oval piece of thick plywood and a large plastic cylinder. The object is to stand and balance on the board as it teeters on the cylinder. The more time spent developing balance and coordination on the Indo Board (or a similar board), the better your surfing.

These exercises can be performed on a daily basis throughout the week without interfering with your other training. As your ability, balance, and coordination on the board improves, traditional strength training exercises can be incorporated (e.g. lateral raise, straight-arm pulldown, triceps pushdown). Ultimately, any exercise that can be performed in a standing posture can be done on the Indo Board.

The sample workouts in the appendix do not include Indo Board training for two reasons: the advanced nature of the exercises and because not everyone owns one. You may purchase an Indo Board online at www.indoboard.com or by calling (321) 724-6823.

These are *very* advanced exercises and should be executed with extreme caution. Before attempting any of them it would be wise to become familiar with the movements of the Indo Board by simply standing on it while trying to maintain your balance. Beginners should have a sturdy post to hold on to due to the potential hazards of the exercises.

There are two types of Indo Boards: the Classic (right) and the Surfer Pro (left).

adv. balance training

Use a support post to maintain your balance the first few times you mount the board.

Standing

1. Place one end of the board on the ground and position the opposite end on the cylinder so that it overlaps the cylinder by a few inches.

2. Place one foot on the end of the board that is touching the ground. [1]

3. Place your other foot on the raised end of the board and press downward. Be sure to keep your knees bent as you transfer your body weight over the cylinder.

4. Keep both knees bent, shoulders above your hips, and your arms relaxed by your side. [2]

5. Do not straighten your legs, lock your knees, or raise your arms to try to balance (although that will be your instinct). Do just the opposite by sinking down into a squat position and bringing your arms down between your knees.

6. Perform 3 to 5 sets of 30 seconds to two minutes.

adv. balance training

Side-to-Side

1. Begin by balancing on the board with your knees bent and your feet positioned near the ends of the board. [1]

2. Slowly sweep your legs from side to side, keeping the cylinder between your feet, until your motion resembles a pendulum. [2]

3. Try to keep your head motionless above the cylinder and your arms relaxed by your sides.

4. Perform 2 to 4 sets of continuous movement for 30 seconds to 1 minute.

adv. balance training

Static Squat

1. Begin by balancing on the board with your knees bent and your feet positioned near the ends of the board.

2. As you lower your body, tilt your pelvis downward and keep your shoulders above your hips.

3. Maintain this squat position with as little movement as possible.

4. Perform 2 to 4 sets of 30 seconds to 1 minute.

Active Squat

1. Begin by balancing on the board with your knees bent and your feet positioned near the ends of the board. [1]

2. Tilt your pelvis downward and keep your shoulders above your hips.

3. Inhale as you lower your body into the squat position. [2]

4. Exhale as you rise back up to the starting position.

5. Perform 2 to 4 sets of 10 to 20 repetitions.

adv. balance training

Split Squat

1. Stand at one end of the board with your shoulders parallel to the long dimension of the cylinder.

2. Position one end of the board so that it overlaps the cylinder by a few inches.

3. Place one foot on the end of the board that is touching the ground. This foot should be parallel to the long dimension of the board.

4. Place your other foot on the raised end of the board and press downward. Be sure to keep your knees bent as you transfer your body weight over the cylinder. [1]

5. Inhale as you lower your body into a split squat. [2]

6. Exhale as you rise back up to the starting position.

7. Perform 2 to 4 sets of 10 to 20 repetitions. Be sure to switch your forward leg with each set.

adv. balance training

Pivoting Split Squat

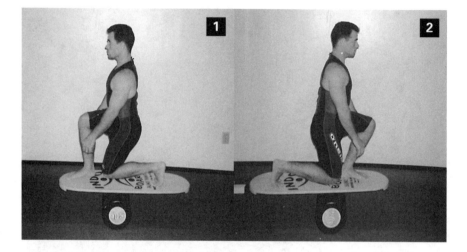

1. Stand at one end of the board with your shoulders parallel to the long dimension of the cylinder.

2. Position one end of the board so that it overlaps the cylinder by a few inches.

3. Place one foot on the end of the board that is touching the ground.

4. Place your other foot on the other end of the board and press downward. Be sure to keep your knees bent as you transfer your body weight over the cylinder.

5. Lower your body into the bottom position of the split squat. [1]

6. Keeping your board balanced and as motionless as possible, exhale as you pivot to your left, on the balls of your feet, until you're facing the opposite direction. [2]

7. Inhale as you pivot and return to the starting position.

8. Perform 2 to 4 sets of 10 to 20 repetitions.

9. Repeat exercise pivoting to the right and back to the starting position.

adv. balance training

Crouch and Pivot

1. The Crouch and Pivot is similar to the Pivoting Split Squat except that your body is lower to the board.

2. For added difficulty, reach your right arm across your body and grab the left front edge of your board. [1]

3. Keeping your board balanced and as motionless as possible, exhale as you pivot on the balls of your feet to your left until you're facing the opposite direction. [2]

4. Exhale as you twist into position to repeat the process going in the opposite direction.

5. Inhale as you return to center and into the static squat position.

6. Perform 2 to 4 sets of 10 to 20 repetitions.

adv. balance training

Nose Ride

1. Begin by balancing on the board.

2. Shift the board under your body until your right foot is above the cylinder. [1]

3. Quickly reposition your left foot to the same edge of the board as your right foot. [2]

4. Maintain balance without letting either edge of the board touch the floor.

5. Step back with your left foot to the starting position.

6. Switch lead foot and repeat.

7. Breathe normally throughout the exercise.

8. Perform 2 to 4 sets of 10 to 20 repetitions.

adv. balance training

Floater

1. Begin by positioning one long side of the board 2 or 3 inches from the end of the cylinder, with most of the cylinder exposed in front of you.

2. Balance on the board in a slight squat position. [1]

3. Twist your hips so the board pivots ninety degrees over and onto the exposed end of the cylinder. [2]

4. Maintain your balance for a few seconds before pivoting the board back to the starting position.

5. Repeat exercise pivoting in the opposite direction.

6. For an added challenge, begin with the board in the normal starting position and "hop" the board backward so it's now just at the edge of the cylinder, behind you. Repeat steps 3-6.

7. Perform 2 to 4 sets of 10 repetitions.

adv. balance training

Chapter 7

Endurance Training

A surfer requires not only flexibility and strength for heavy paddling but also muscular endurance to maintain stamina for an entire surf session. In creating an effective endurance program of cardiovascular activities, four elements are critical.

Increasing or upgrading any one of these elements will increase the demands placed on your body as it works to develop the cardiovascular fitness essential to endurance.

These elements are:

- Frequency: The number of times the endurance exercise is performed in a particular period of time.

- Duration: The length of time it takes to perform the exercise.

- Intensity: The effort level reached during the exercise.

- Type: The choice of exercise performed in a workout.

The following are cardiovascular exercises that are either specific to surfing or can serve as cross-training activities (such as stair climbing or running). The detailed programs in chapter 9 include these exercises and offer recommendations on duration and intensity of the workouts.

It's helpful at this point to understand the *overload principle*—

the general idea that by overloading or exhausting muscles in a careful, systematic manner, physiological changes will occur that make the muscles stronger and more durable. A man who performs as many push-ups as he possibly can each day will eventually grow stronger, because he has regularly taxed his muscles to a point of fatigue. This principle will come into play as you develop a program of increasingly rigorous endurance activities.

Paddling

It may sound obvious, but to become a stronger paddling machine, a surfer needs to paddle. A simple way to vary the intensity of your paddling workouts is to use boards of different lengths. A short surfboard is less buoyant than a longer surfboard, creating more drag as you move through the water and requiring more effort to paddle. For training, you can start with a longer board and progress to shorter boards to increase the intensity of the workouts.

Resistance Paddling

Get a plastic bucket with a sturdy handle, or use a large coffee can. Drill holes in the container until it looks like Swiss cheese. Simply tie the container to your ankle leash.

The bucket adds tremendous resistance as you paddle your board. The fewer holes you drill, the more resistance you'll feel as you work to paddle against the dead weight of the water-filled bucket.

Partner Towing

With a surfing friend, take turns towing each other on the surfboard by holding onto the other person's ankle leash. You can count the number of strokes and then switch leads when you reach a particular number. You might also choose to change positions after an interval time of 1 to 5 minutes or a distance of 50 to 150 yards.

Land Paddle with Resistance Bands

When the weather turns nasty but you still want a paddle workout, you can make use of a rubber resistance band (preferably one with handles). They're available at sporting goods stores.

Secure the middle of the band to an immovable object (such as a table leg) a few feet off the ground. Hold on to both ends of the resistance band, kneel or lie face down on a flat padded bench, and mimic the motions of surfboard paddling. The farther the bench is placed away from the band's point of attachment, the more resistance you'll be working against. Check for wear in the band and replace it if you find any tear or abrasion; you don't want it to break, snapping back at you.

Swimming

Swimming is great cross-training exercise for surfers—and if your leash snaps or you're not wearing one, swimming can become very important! It may be a good idea to take a few lessons at your local swim center if you are unfamiliar with proper form.

Underwater Swimming

Surfers should be able to hold their breath underwater for prolonged periods of time, especially when surfing bigger waves. It's important to train the lungs and the mind to be able to stay underwater, without panicking, while swimming back to the surface.

Wear a watch to keep track of your times when swimming underwater. Start with intervals of 15 to 30 seconds and slowly add more time with each workout. For safety, make these sessions close to shore or in a pool.

Other Methods of Endurance Training

Stair Climbing

Cross-training with stair-climbing machines at health clubs can provide a good workout. But if there is a long flight of stairs in your neighborhood—preferably of wood rather than unforgiving concrete—try going up and down these for an endurance workout.

When climbing stairs, maintain the same form as in running or walking: stand tall. Walk slowly on the way down to allow your body and heart rate to recover.

Walking and Running

Whether you walk or run doesn't really matter: you'll reach the same destination eventually. It just might take more time if you walk. They are both good choices as part of an endurance training routine.

Whichever you choose, stand as tall as possible. Keep your head over your shoulders; chest up, and hips tucked under. Let the arms swing freely forward and backward, and keep your feet pointing straight ahead.

Rowing Machine

Indoor rowing machines such as those used at commercial gyms provide a great full-body workout and a terrific cross-training exercise. Be sure to maintain good seated posture at all times. Use the legs as much as possible, because they have the body's biggest muscles. Exhale when pulling the handle inward.

Chapter 8

Surf Team Drills

Most of this book focuses on what an individual can do to become a stronger, fitter surfer. This chapter is devoted to drills for surf teams or other groups. It's important to build camaraderie within a team, a good reason for training together. Working in a group is also a great way to stay motivated. When strength training, try to pair up members who have similar strength levels so they can act as spotters for each other during the exercises.

Following are some team and group conditioning drills for both water and land. These drills can be scheduled on endurance training days or on the off days. They are meant to be challenging yet fun.

Drafting Paddle

Most moving objects create a draft, pulling energy toward the back of the object from behind. The field of energy behind the object allows the objects following the first to use less effort while maintaining the same velocity. Bike racers and runners often use drafting as a technique to allow those in the back a bit of a rest. In this drill the technique is applied to surfers. For this drill, choose a distance such as 1 mile, half-mile, or quarter-mile. Start with a short distance and increase it as the group becomes better conditioned.

Have the surfers line up on their boards one behind the other in a straight line. The lead surfer begins to paddle almost as hard as he or she can, with the rest close behind. The last surfer in line has to break away from the line and overtake the leader. As soon as this last surfer takes the lead position, the surfer that is now the farthest back must battle hard to take the lead.

Continue the drill until the desired distance is covered.

Drafting Runs and Cycling

You can use the same routine as in the Drafting Paddle drill for running or cycling in a group. Form a straight line and take off. The last person must overtake the leader. Continue this process of catch-the-leader until a desired time or distance is reached.

For safety reasons choose a route with little or no traffic. It may be a good idea to run or cycle on a track or run in a park or forest.

Paddle Relays

Divide the group into two teams. Half the surfers in Team A and half the surfers in Team B remain at the starting line, while the rest get in position at a turnaround point 50 to 100 yards away.

As the whistle blows to start the relay, one surfer from Team A and one from Team B paddle as hard as they can to reach and tag a teammate at the turnaround. Once tagged, a paddler races as hard as possible back to the starting line to tag another compatriot, who then takes off. Continue the relay until the last surfer finishes.

For added incentive, have a prize for the winning squad. For instance, give winners the choice of waves during surfing practice.

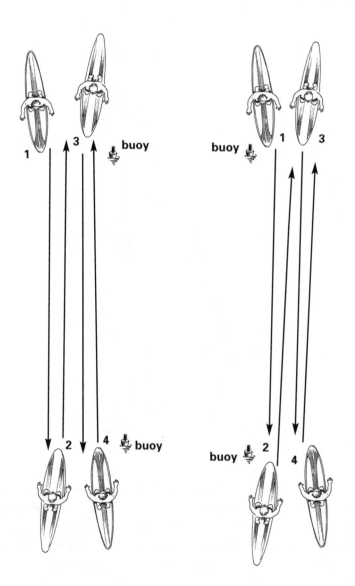

Suicide Drills

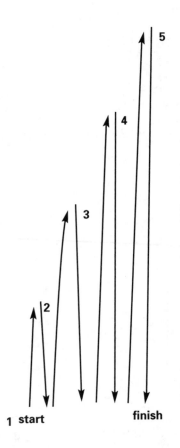

Set up five solid markers on the beach in a straight, evenly spaced row that totals about 40 yards. These five markers can be most anything: rocks, flags, pieces of driftwood—even lines in the sand. Team members must sprint from the first marker to the second and back to the first. Then sprint to the third marker and back to the first without stopping. Then to the fourth marker and back to the first. Then finally to the fifth marker and back.

Allow 2 minutes of recovery time before the group begins the next set. Perform 3 to 4 sets.

You can carry out the same drill while paddling on the water, using flotation devices spaced 10 to 20 yards apart.

Water Sprints

In knee-high water, team members sprint on foot for 20 to 40 yards. Allow 1 to 2 minutes of recovery time before beginning the next set. Be sure the running surface is level and free of rocks and reef for safety reasons. This drill can also be done on soft sand or set up as a relay to keep things interesting.

Chapter 9

Sample Workout Programs

Now that all the components of the paddler's conditioning program have been discussed in detail it is time to put your program together. The sample workouts given in this chapter will help you create your program. The workouts each have three parts: flexibility, endurance, and strength. Although the flexibility portion appears first remember that most gains occur when stretching is performed at the end of a workout. The routines are made up of lying, sitting, kneeling, and standing stretches. Be sure to select a few stretches from each group with each program you design. Also the Sun Salutation is not included with the samples. Instead use the Sun Salutation as a wake-up routine as often as possible. It will increase your flexibility and energize you first thing in the morning.

The endurance program is a blend of land and water exercises. Depending on weather and water conditions, at times you may be forced to use more land endurance exercises but if possible create a blend. Labels of "Low," "Moderate," and "High" are given to describe the intensity level of an exercise. "Low" refers to 60-70 percent of maximum heart rate and 5-6 on the scale of the Rate of Perceived Exertion (RPE). "Moderate" is 70-80 percent of maximum heart rate and 6-7 on the RPE scale. "High" refers to 80-90 percent of maximum heart rate and 7-9 on the RPE scale.

The strength program is a combination of upper body, lower body, and torso exercises. Stability ball and medicine ball exercises are also included. If you have the use of these exercise balls incorporate them into your routine as often as possible. If not, create as much variety in the other exercises as possible. Focus on the exercises that are challenging. Too often people focus on the exercises that are their "strong suits." They perform these exercises more than any others which creates strength imbalances (one muscle stronger than its counterpart). Imbalances lead to improper movement, and improper movements increase the chance of injury. Part of this approach is to *find* the exercises that are challenging. The true challenge is not to bench press 300 pounds; rather it is to find the weaker muscles and improve their strength.

Not all exercises appearing in this book are included in the sample routines. I didn't want you to simply copy my routines. Be original! Be creative! Hopefully enough variety and information has been provided so you can create your own program. Refer as often as you like to the photos and descriptions of the various exercises earlier in the book. The flexibility exercises are in chapter 2; strength exercises in chapter 4; medicine ball and stability ball exercises in chapter 5; and endurance exercises in chapter 7. See appendix 1 for a list of all exercises. See the index to locate the page number for a specific exercise.

Home Program

Gyms and health clubs aren't your cup of tea? Too many muscleheads? Too much fluorescent spandex? Whatever the issue don't worry, you do not have to join the sweatshops. The following sample routines can be performed in the comfort and privacy of your home. It may not be a bad idea to invest in a few dumbbells, a medicine ball, and perhaps a stability ball. This will increase the number of exercises you can choose from.

Home Program: Weeks 1 and 2

Flexibility Training: 3–6 days per week

Exercise	Time
Crossed Knee Lift	30 sec.
Crossover Twist	30 sec.
Mad Cat Stretch	30 sec.
Lateral Neck Stretch	30 sec.
Forward Neck Stretch	30 sec.

Strength Training: 3–4 days per week

Exercise	Set 1/ Repetitions	Set 2/ Repetitions	Set 3/ Repetitions
Abdominal Crunch	20 reps	20 reps	25 reps
Oblique Crunch	20 reps	20 reps	25 reps
Push-up (knees)	15 reps	15 reps	15 reps
Burpees	15 reps	15 reps	15 reps
Horizontal Pull-up	15 reps	12 reps	10 reps
Reverse Dumbbell Fly	15 reps	15 reps	15 reps
Squat (body weight)	15 reps	15 reps	15 reps
Forward Lunge (body weight)	10 reps	10 reps	10 reps
Seated Twist (medicine ball)	15 reps	15 reps	15 reps
Abdominal Crunch (stability ball)	15 reps	15 reps	15 reps

Endurance Training: 2–3 days per week

Exercise	Time	Intensity	Frequency
Paddling (longboard)	20 min.	Medium	2 times a week
Walking	30 min.	Low	2 times a week

Home Program: Weeks 3 and 4

Flexibility Training: 3–6 days per week

Exercise	Time
Crossed Knee Lift	30 sec.
Crossover Twist	30 sec.
Mad Cat Stretch	30 sec.
Lateral Neck Stretch	30 sec.
Forward Neck Stretch	30 sec.

Strength Training: 3-4 days per week

Exercise	Set 1/ Repetitions	Set 2/ Repetitions	Set 3/ Repetitions
Oblique Crunch	25 reps	25 reps	25 reps
Lower-back Exercise	20 reps	20 reps	20 reps
Push-up (toes)	15 reps	15 reps	15 reps
Bench Dip	15 reps	15 reps	15 reps
Dumbbell Pullover	15 reps	15 reps	15 reps
External Rotation I	15 reps	15 reps	15 reps
Split Squat (body weight)	15 reps	15 reps	15 reps
Reverse Lunge (body weight)	15 reps	15 reps	15 reps
Wall Sit	30 sec.	30 sec.	30 sec.
Overhead Toss (medicine ball)	15 reps	15 reps	15 reps
Push-up (stability ball)	15 reps	15 reps	15 reps

Endurance Training: 2-3 days per week

Exercise	Time	Intensity	Frequency
Paddling (short board)	20 min.	Medium	3 times a week
Stair Climbing	20 min.	Medium	2 times a week

Home Program: Weeks 5 and 6

Flexibility Training: 3–6 days per week

Exercise	Time
Crossed Knee Lift	30 sec.
Crossover Twist	30 sec.
Mad Cat Stretch	30 sec.
Arm Circles	45 sec.
Shoulder Pivots	45 sec.

Strength Training: 3–4 days per week

Exercise	Set 1/ Repetitions	Set 2/ Repetitions	Set 3/ Repetitions
Abdominal Crunch	25 reps	25 reps	25 reps
Supine Eagles	20 reps	20 reps	20 reps
Popping Push-up	15 reps	15 reps	15 reps
Burpees	10 reps	12 reps	15 reps
Horizontal Pull-up	15 reps	15 reps	15 reps
Reverse Dumbbell Fly	15 reps	15 reps	15 reps
Squat (dumbbells)	15 reps	12 reps	10 reps
Wall Sit	45 sec.	45 sec.	45 sec.
Rotary Torso Toss (medicine ball)	15 reps	15 reps	15 reps
Torso Rotation (stability ball)	15 reps	15 reps	15 reps

Exercise	Time	Intensity	Frequency
Resistance Paddling (longboard)	30 min.	High	3 times a week
Running	30 min.	Medium	2 times a week

Home Program: Weeks 7 and 8

Flexibility Training: 3–6 days per week

Exercise	Time
Crossed Knee Lift	30 sec.
Downward-facing Dog	45 sec.
Crossover Twist	30 sec.
Mad Cat Stretch	30 sec.
Crossed Arm Stretch	45 sec.
Shoulder Pivots	45 sec.

Strength Training: 3–4 days per week

Exercise	Set 1/ Repetitions	Set 2/ Repetitions	Set 3/ Repetitions
Lower-back Exercise	20 reps	20 reps	20 reps
Abdominal Crunch	30 reps	30 reps	30 reps
Hanging Leg Lift	20 reps	20 reps	20 reps
Push-up on Balance Board	10 reps	10 reps	10 reps
Bench Dip	20 reps	15 reps	10 reps
Pull-up	10 reps	8 reps	8 reps
Dumbbell Pullover	15 reps	12 reps	10 reps
Split Squat (body weight)	15 reps	15 reps	15 reps
Reverse Lunge (body weight)	15 reps	15 reps	15 reps
Squat (dumbbells)	15 reps	12 reps	12 reps
Seated Twist (medicine ball)	15 reps	15 reps	15 reps
Back Extension with Twist (stability ball)	15 reps	15 reps	15 reps

Endurance Training: 2–3 days per week

Exercise	Time	Intensity	Frequency
Partner Towing	10 reps/1 min.	High	2 times a week
Stair Climbing	25 min.	Medium	2 times a week
Underwater Swimming	10 reps/20 sec.	Medium	2 times a week

Home Program: Weeks 9 and 10

Flexibility Training: 3–6 days per week

Exercise	Time
Arm Circles	1 min.
Mad Cat Stretch	1 min.
Forward Neck Stretch	45 sec.
Lateral Neck Stretch	45 sec.
Downward-facing Dog	1 min.
Shoulder Pivots	1 min.
Quadriceps Stretch	45 sec.

Strength Training: 3–4 days per week

Exercise	Set 1/ Repetitions	Set 2/ Repetitions	Set 3/ Repetitions
Hanging Leg Lift	20 reps	25 reps	25 reps
Supine Eagles	30 reps	30 reps	30 reps
Abdominal Crunch	30 reps	30 reps	30 reps
Plyometric Push-up	10 reps	10 reps	10 reps
Burpees	20 reps	15 reps	10 reps
Reverse Dumbbell Fly	15 reps	15 reps	15 reps
External Rotation I	15 reps	15 reps	15 reps
Wall Sit	1 min.	1 min.	1 min.
Walking Lunge (body weight)	20 reps	20 reps	20 reps
Chest Pass Crunch (medicine ball)	15 reps	15 reps	15 reps
Push-up (stability ball)	15 reps	15 reps	15 reps

Exercise	Time	Intensity	Frequency
Resistance Paddling (short board)	10 reps/1 min.	High	2 times a week
Running	40 min.	Medium	2 times a week
Underwater Swimming	10 reps/30 sec.	Medium	2 times a week

Gym Program

Are you a member of a gym? Thinking of joining one in the near future? The following routines are samples of what your gym routine might look like. Some machines may look different than the ones featured in this book. If you are unsure of the equipment be certain to ask a staff member for help.

One more thing: gym etiquette. Please carry a workout towel to wipe your perspiration off machines and allow other members to share equipment you are using when you are between sets. Your fellow gym members will thank you.

Gym Program: Weeks 1 and 2

Flexibility Training: 3–6 days per week

Exercise	Time
Crossed Knee Lift	30 sec.
Crossover Twist	30 sec.
Mad Cat Stretch	30 sec.
Forward Neck Stretch	30 sec.
Lateral Neck Stretch	30 sec.

Strength Training: 3–4 days per week

Exercise	Set 1/ Repetitions	Set 2/ Repetitions	Set 3/ Repetitions
Abdominal Crunch	20 reps	20 reps	20 reps
Oblique Crunch	20 reps	20 reps	20 reps
Push-up (knees)	15 reps	15 reps	15 reps
Bench Press (dumbbells)	15 reps	12 reps	10 reps
Lat Pulldown	15 reps	12 reps	10 reps
External Rotation I	15 reps	15 reps	15 reps
Squat (dumbbells)	15 reps	12 reps	10 reps
Split Squat (body weight)	15 reps	15 reps	15 reps
Russian Twist (medicine ball)	15 reps	15 reps	15 reps
Abdominal Crunch (stability ball)	15 reps	15 reps	15 reps

Endurance Training: 2–3 days per week

Exercise	Time	Intensity	Frequency
Paddling (longboard)	20 min.	Medium	2 times a week
Walking	30 min.	Low	2 times a week

Gym Program: Weeks 3 and 4

Excercise/Flexibility Training: 3–6 days per week

Time	Time
Arm Circles	30 sec.
Shoulder Pivots	30 sec.
Crossed Knee Lift	30 sec.
Crossover Twist	30 sec.
Mad Cat Stretch	30 sec.

Strength Training: 3–4 days per week

Exercise	Set 1/ Repetitions	Set 2/ Repetitions	Set 3/ Repetitions
Abdominal Crunch	20 reps	25 reps	30 reps
Supine Eagles	20 reps	20 reps	20 reps
Push-up (toes)	15 reps	15 reps	15 reps
Bench Press (barbell)	15 reps	12 reps	10 reps
Straight-arm Pulldown	15 reps	12 reps	10 reps
Dumbbell Pullover	15 reps	15 reps	12 reps
External Rotation I	15 reps	15 reps	15 reps
Squat (barbell)	15 reps	12 reps	10 reps
Split Squat (barbell)	15 reps	12 reps	10 reps
Overhead Toss (medicine ball)	15 reps	15 reps	15 reps
Back Extension (stability ball)	15 reps	15 reps	15 reps

Endurance Training: 2–3 days per week

Exercise	Time	Intensity	Frequency
Paddling (longboard)	30 min.	Medium	2 times a week
Running	30 min.	Medium	2 times a week

Gym Program: Weeks 5 and 6

Flexibility Training: 3–6 days per week

Exercise	Time
Crossed Arm Stretch	30 sec.
Chest and Shoulder Stretch	30 sec.
Crossed Knee Lift	45 sec.
Crossover Twist	45 sec.
Mad Cat Stretch	45 sec.

Strength Training: 3-4 days per week

Exercise	Set 1/ Repetitions	Set 2/ Repetitions	Set 3/ Repetitions
Oblique Crunch	25 reps	25 reps	25 reps
Lower-back Exercise	20 reps	20 reps	20 reps
Push-up on Balance Board	15 reps	15 reps	15 reps
Bench Dip	15 reps	15 reps	15 reps
Horizontal Pull-up	15 reps	12 reps	10 reps
One-arm Row	15 reps	12 reps	10 reps
Walking Lunge (body weight)	20 reps	20 reps	20 reps
Squat (dumbbells)	15 reps	15 reps	12 reps
Wall Sit	1 min.	30 sec.	30 sec.
Seated Twist (medicine ball)	15 reps	15 reps	15 reps
Push-up (stability ball)	15 reps	15 reps	15 reps

Endurance Training: 2-3 days per week

Exercise	Time	Intensity	Frequency
Paddling (short board)	30 min.	Medium	2 times a week
Stair Climbing	20 min.	Medium	2 times a week

Gym Program: Weeks 7 and 8

Flexibility Training: 3–6 days per week

Exercise	Time
Crossed Knee Lift	1 min.
Crossover Twist	1 min.
Mad Cat Stretch	45 sec.
Downward-facing Dog	1 min.
Lateral Neck Stretch	45 sec.

Strength Training: 3–4 days per week

Exercise	Set 1/ Repetitions	Set 2/ Repetitions	Set 3/ Repetitions
Hanging Leg Lift	20 reps	25 reps	25 reps
Abdominal Crunch	30 reps	30 reps	30 reps
Popping Push-up	12 reps	12 reps	12 reps
Burpees	12 reps	12 reps	12 reps
Pull-up	12 reps	12 reps	10 reps
Reverse Dumbbell Fly	15 reps	12 reps	10 reps
Walking Lunge (dumbbells)	16 reps	12 reps	10 reps
Reverse Lunge (barbell)	15 reps	12 reps	10 reps
Split Squat (barbell)	15 reps	12 reps	8 reps
Rotary Torso Toss (medicine ball)	15 reps	15 reps	15 reps
Back Extension with Twist (stability ball)	15 reps	15 reps	15 reps

Endurance Training: 2–3 days per week

Exercise	Time	Intensity	Frequency
Resistance Paddling	20 min.	High	2 times a week
Rowing Machine	20 min.	Medium	2 times a week
Underwater Swimming	10 reps/30 sec.	Medium	2 times a week

Gym Program: Weeks 9 and 10

Flexibility Training: 3–6 days per week

Exercise	Time
Arm Circles	1 min.
Shoulder Pivots	1 min.
Quadriceps Stretch	45 sec.
Mad Cat Stretch	1 min.
Forward Neck Stretch	45 sec.
Downward-facing Dog	1 min.
Lateral Neck Stretch	45 sec.

Strength Training: 3–4 days per week

Exercise	Set 1/ Repetitions	Set 2/ Repetitions	Set 3/ Repetitions
Hanging Leg Lift	30 reps	30 reps	30 reps
Supine Eagles	30 reps	30 reps	30 reps
Abdominal Crunch	30 reps	30 reps	30 reps
Plyometric Push-up	12 reps	12 reps	12 reps
Bench Press (barbell)	15 reps	12 reps	10 reps
Lat Pulldown	15 reps	15 reps	15 reps
Triceps Pushdown	15 reps	15 reps	12 reps
Wall Sit	1 min.	1 min.	1 min.
Split Squat (dumbbells)	16 reps	12 reps	10 reps
Squat (barbell)	15 reps	12 reps	10 reps
Chest Pass Crunch (medicine ball)	15 reps	15 reps	15 reps
Trunk Rotation (stability ball)	15 reps	15 reps	15 reps

Endurance Training: 2–3 days per week

Exercise	Time	Intensity	Frequency
Partner Towing	10 reps/1 min.	High	2 times a week
Swimming	40 min.	Medium	2 times a week
Underwater Swimming	10 reps/30 sec.	Medium	2 times a week

Appendix 1

Exercises at a Glance

Following is a list of all exercises described in this book, categorized by whether they are aimed mainly at promoting flexibility, strength, or endurance. You can use this list in personalizing your workouts, selecting from a variety of these exercises in adapting the workout programs in chapter 9 to suit your particular conditioning goals.

Check the chapters indicated in order to review the photos and descriptions of any of these exercises.

Flexibility Exercises (choose 2 to 4)

In chapter 2:

Crossed Knee Lift
Crossover Twist
Mad Cat Stretch
Chest and Shoulder Stretch
Seated Torso Twist
Simple Twist
Seated Lower-Back Stretch
Bar Hang
Crossed Arm Stretch
Arm Circles
Shoulder Pivots
Lateral Neck Stretch

Forward Neck Stretch
Triangle Pose
Reverse Triangle Pose
Advanced Shoulder Stretch
Warrior Pose
Side Reach
Upper Spinal Floor Twist
Upward-Facing Dog
Downward-Facing Dog
Quadriceps Stretch

In chapter 3:

Sun Salutation (series of stretches)

Strength Exercises

Upper-Body Exercises (choose 3 to 5)

In chapter 4:

Push-Up on the Knees
Push-Up on the Toes
Push-Up on Balance Board
Plyometric Push-Up on Balance Board
Bench Press
Lat Pulldown
Bench Dip
Pull-Up
Straight-Arm Pulldown
Horizontal Pull-Up
Single Straight-Arm Pulldown
Dumbbell Pullover

One-Arm Row
Reverse Dumbbell Fly
Bent-Over Row
Triceps Pushdown
External Rotation I
External Rotation II

In chapter 5:
Push-Up (on stability ball)

In chapter 6 (skill transfer):
Burpees
Popping Push-Up

Lower-body Exercises (choose 3 to 5)

Squats and lunges can be performed with weights (barbell or dumbbells) or with body weight only.

In chapter 4:
Squat
Split Squat
Forward Lunge
Reverse Lunge
Walking Lunge
Wall Sit

Torso Exercises (choose 2 to 4)

In chapter 4:
The Chop
Abdominal Crunch
Twisting Lift
Oblique Crunch
Opposite Arm and Leg Raise
Lateral Torso Lift
Bicycles

In chapter 5 (medicine ball):
Seated Twist
Russian Twist
Overhead Toss
Rotary Torso Toss
Chest Pass Crunch

In chapter 5 (stability ball):
Abdominal Crunch
Trunk (Torso) Rotation
Back Extension
Back Extension with Twist

In chapter 6 (skill transfer):
Hanging Leg Lift
Supine Eagles
Standing Torso Rotation

Endurance Exercises (choose 1 to 3)

In chapter 7:

Resistance Paddling
Partner Towing
Land Paddle with Resistance
    Bands
Underwater Swimming
Stair Climbing
Walking and Running
Rowing Machine

In chapter 8 (team drills):

Drafting Paddle
Drafting Runs and Cycling
Paddle Relays
Suicide Drills
Water Sprints

Workout Log

Rocky's Functional Integrative Training

| Workout #1 | Workout #2 | Workout #3 |

Cardiovascular Conditioning   Target Heart Rate = _____ beats/min.

Type of exercise	prog	int	dur	Type of exercise	prog	int	dur	Type of exercise	prog	int	dur
1 PADDLE - LONGBOARD	LOW	30 min		1 PADDLE - SHORTBOARD	MED	30 min		1 PADDLE - INTERVAL	HIGH	30 min	
2 WALKING	LOW	30 min		2 RUNNING	HIGH	30 min		2 UNDERWATER SWIM	MED	15 min	
3				3				3 ROWING MACHINE	MED	20 min	

Strength Training   ____ sets x ____ reps

Type of exercise	set1	set2	set3	Type of exercise	set1	set2	set3	Type of exercise	set1	set2	set3
1 ABDOMINAL CRUNCH	BODY/25	BODY/25	BODY/25	1 BICYCLES	BODY/20	BODY/20	BODY/20	1 HANGING LEG LIFT	BODY/20	BODY/15	BODY/12
2 OBLIQUE CRUNCH	BODY/20	BODY/20	BODY/20	2 SUPINE EAGLES	BODY/20	BODY/20	BODY/20	2 ABDOMINAL CRUNCH	BODY/15	BODY/12	BODY/10
3 PUSH UPS ON KNEES	BODY/15	BODY/12	BODY/10	3 PUSH UPS ON TOES	BODY/15	BODY/12	BODY/10	3 POPPING PUSH UPS	BODY/15	BODY/12	BODY/10
4 DUMBBELL BENCH PRESS	20/15	25/12	30/10	4 PLYOMETRIC PUSH UPS	BODY/10	BODY/10	BODY/10	4 BURPEES	BODY/15	BODY/12	BODY/10
5 LAT PULLDOWN	50/15	60/12	70/10	5 STRAIGHT ARM PULLDOWN	40/15	50/15	60/12	5 PULL UP	BODY/10	BODY/8	BODY/8
6 EXTERNAL ROTATION	3/15	3/15	5/12	6 DUMBBELL PULLOVER	30/15	35/15	40/12	6 REVERSE FLY	5/15	8/12	10/10
7 DUMBBELL SQUAT	15/15	20/12	25/10	7 EXTERNAL ROTATION	3/15	5/12	5/12	7 FRONT LUNGE	BODY/15	10/12	15/10
8 SPLIT SQUAT	10/15	15/12	20/10	8 SQUAT	45/15	55/12	65/10	8 REVERSE LUNGE	BODY/15	10/12	15/10
9				9 WALKING LUNGE	5/15	8/15	10/15	9 SPLIT SQUAT	BODY/15	10/12	15/10
10				10				10			

Flexibility Training   hold each pose for 1-3 x 10-20 sec.

Workout #1	Workout #2	Workout #3
1 CROSSED KNEE LIFT	1 I.T. BAND STRETCH W/STRAP	1 UPPER SPINAL FLOOR TWIST
2 CROSSOVER TWIST	2 CALF STRETCH W/STRAP	2 SHOULDER PIVOTS
3 HAMSTRING STRETCH W/STRAP	3 CROCODILE TWIST	3 ARM CIRCLES
4 CROSSED ARM STRETCH	4 SHOULDER PIVOTS	4 BOAT POSE
5 ARM CIRCLES	5 MODIFIED SHOULDER STAND	5 SEATED LOW BACK STRETCH
6 MODIFIED HURDLER'S STRETCH	6 SIMPLE TWIST	6 BAR HANG
7 TRIANGLE POSE	7 CHEST/SHOULDER STRETCH	7 WARRIOR POSE
8 DOWNWARD DOG	8 DOWNWARD DOG	8 TRIANGLE POSE

Rocky's Functional Integrative Training

Workout #1	Workout #2	Workout #3

Cardiovascular Conditioning   Target Heart Rate = ____ beats/min.

Type of exercise	prog	int	dur	Type of exercise	prog	int	dur	Type of exercise	prog	int	dur
1				1				1			
2				2				2			
3				3				3			

Strength Training   ____ sets x ____ reps

Type of exercise	set1	set2	set3	Type of exercise	set1	set2	set3	Type of exercise	set1	set2	set3
1				1				1			
2				2				2			
3				3				3			
4				4				4			
5				5				5			
6				6				6			
7				7				7			
8				8				8			
9				9				9			
10				10				10			

Flexibility Training   hold each pose for 1-3 x 10-20 sec.

1	1	1
2	2	2
3	3	3
4	4	4
5	5	5
6	6	6
7	7	7
8	8	8

Appendix 3

Resources

Alter, Michael J. *Sport Stretch*. 2nd ed. Champaign IL: Human Kinetics, 1998.

Baechle, Thomas R., and Roger Earle, eds. *Essentials of Strength Training and Conditioning*. 2nd ed. Champaign IL: Human Kinetics, 2000.

Couch, Jean. *The Runner's Yoga Book: A Balanced Approach to Fitness*. Berkeley: Rodmell Press, 1990.

Horrigan, Joseph, D.C., and Jerry Robinson. *The 7-Minute Rotator Cuff Solution*. Los Angeles: Health for Life, 1991.

Muscle Balance and Function Development, www.dpdc-mbf.com

Appendix 4

Muscle Chart

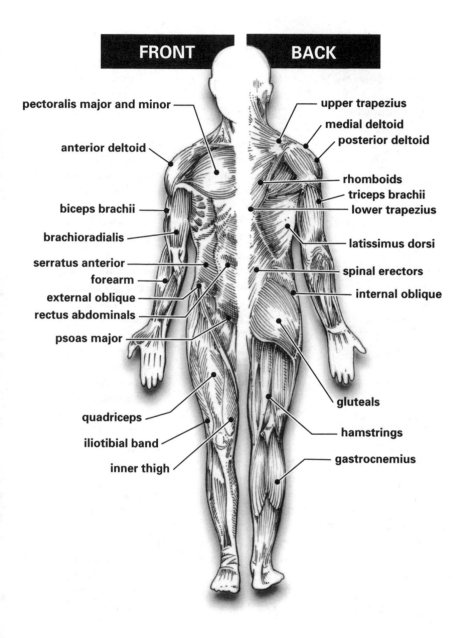

FRONT

BACK

pectoralis major and minor

anterior deltoid

biceps brachii

brachioradialis

serratus anterior

forearm

external oblique

rectus abdominals

psoas major

quadriceps

iliotibial band

inner thigh

upper trapezius

medial deltoid

posterior deltoid

rhomboids

triceps brachii

lower trapezius

latissimus dorsi

spinal erectors

internal oblique

gluteals

hamstrings

gastrocnemius

Index